Eighty from the Eighties

THE *PENINSULA VOICE* INTERVIEWS

Martin Val Baker

RAINYDAY PUBLICATIONS. FIRST EDITION 1993.

ISBN No 0-9506263-1-7
PUBLISHED BY RAINYDAY PUBLICATIONS, CROSS STREET, PENZANCE, CORNWALL.
TELEPHONE: (0736) 66077

PRINTED BY NEW HEADLAND PRINTERS, BREAD STREET, PENZANCE.
SCANNED AND RESET BY THE SCRIPTORIUM, 10 BOWLING GREEN TERRACE, ST IVES.

Contents

These interviews were written for *Peninsula Voice*, a monthly magazine published from Penzance, during the period from 1983 (when the *Voice* had been going for a year) up until 1991. The subjects reflect the enthusiasm of the contributors at the time, and the amount of words, the time or space available on copy night! This book cannot claim to be a comprehensive list; there are many obvious omissions, but it does give an idea of what was going on in the artistic community of West Cornwall during the nineteen-eighties.

Thanks to the Interviewers and especially to Roy Walker who (due to illness) had to interview himself. The other interviews were conducted by Sue Monro, Mike Venning, Martin Val Baker, Ashley Peters, Annette Robinson, Pam Otto, Mike Sagar Fenton, Dave Scott, Carole Bishop, Mercedes Kemp, Greg Palmer, Jody Stewart, Lu Simmons, Kate Vaughan, Bob Devereux and Martin Green. Thanks also to the *Peninsula Voice* Editorial Collective 1982-88 and to Peter Wright Davies for keeping the magazine going.

INTRODUCTION

Sometimes, the only way to get your name into a good book is to write the intro.

And a good book this one is. Where else would you find bedded between the same sheets such varied personalities as Patrick Heron, Sylvia Kantaris, Bert Jansch, Terry Frost, Molly Parkin, Lord St Levan, Max Barrett, and the late, great Cloggy Mellor?

To be interviewed is to bare yourself before the beast under conditions where the risk of veering head first into Pseud's Corner is high.

But this collection of interviews, drawn from over one hundred issues of the splendidly resilient magazine *Peninsula Voice*, steers well clear of the twin reefs of blurb and bombast. Its subjects have a genuine celebrity in the best meaning of that hackneyed word. They could not have wished for more honest interlocutors.

Peninsula Voice gained notoriety because of its refreshing cheekiness. The magazine gained stature also because of its intelligent though sometimes irreverent critique of red-nosed local 'politics'. It was a welcome antithesis to the great car-boot sale of the 'Eighties and to an ill-judged commercialism that viewed West Cornwall as a shopping precinct in Basildon. That *PV* soldiered on for years in the rough old hands of a genuinely rough old pro, Peter Wright Davies, makes it a celebration rather than a publication.

Most contemporary journalism is ephemeral, and much of it is appalling. But newspapers and magazines serve as contemporary mirrors and *The Voice* reflects well. It was always crammed with lively and informed writing by a gang of bright and enthusiastic contributors. They did it all for nothing and certainly not for glory. Out of this torrent of chattering there emerged a lively coverage of local culture. It included regular profiles of the aspiring and the accomplished in the arts, in entertainment, and in public life, as well as focussing on visiting musicians, many of international stature. The collected profiles of this book comprise an excellent record of such stars, toilers and birds of passage.

Most of the interviews were conducted by Sue Monro, Martin Val Baker and Mike Venning. Many others, including Ashley Peters, contributed. All the writers are enthusiastic yet workmanlike and their interviews represent unadorned journalism rather than art criticism.

There is no verbal sparring between interviewer and subject of the kind favoured by national features editors. There is not too much art-babble either to confuse the philistines amongst us. The interviewers have a genuine curiosity about their subjects, and the sympathetic understanding of Sue Monro, Val Baker's insight and Venning's informed judgement are ideally suited to the job.

The portraits are the book's most powerful theme. Ashley Peters is an artist within the community he portrays so vividly. His stock is rising and deservedly so. In these portraits the reason for that is clear. Peters observes his subjects with the minimum of intrusion and works with a deceptive speed. The result is some of the finest portraiture around. It neither undermines nor underpins but, instead, captures the subject's naturalness free from posture and uncertainty.

Most of those featured in this book will be delighted by their portraits. Some may wince at things recklessly said or at past opinions now abandoned. But that's the price of chattering and the lesson of history. Overall, *Eighty from the 'Eighties* is a splendid gallery of the good if not entirely the great. It is a remarkable record of a region's culture and of its working community of creative people who got their names into this good book on merit rather than introductions ...

DES HANNIGAN
September 1993

Martha Allen

Ashley Peters (June 1988)

"I am trying to uncover feminine myths that have been buried and trying to place women back into art as strong beings rather than decorative creatures."

These words from Martha Allen, ceramicist/sculptress, underpin her present work now on show at The Salthouse Gallery, St Ives, until 3rd June. Born in 1952 in London, she works in Bath and has had several exhibitions in that city since graduating from Bath Academy in 1980. One of 7 children, she has been interested in the arts from an early age, continuing a family tradition,

Her grandfather lived at Bushey, Herts, which was an artists' colony formed in 1883 which was an equivalent of the Newlyn colony of the 1880s. A lot of members of the Newlyn School also had a foot in at Bushey. The grandfather was a woodwork teacher who made puppets and their sets. Martha now, alongside her ceramic/sculpture work, is also a puppet-maker, puppeteer, dancer and folk singer, puppeteering at summer festivals. Her father is a sculptor in his own right, but his work is very different, having no allegorical or searching literary references.

At college, she started off making coiled pots, but soon graduated to producing strange ceramic mythical beasts. It is important to note she started college with a son of two years old to look after as well! Having a child had a bearing on her work.

After art school she had a nervous breakdown which made her read Jungian philosophy to find out what was going on inside herself. She wanted to put some structure on things, to be earthed. Stability is important to her and fed her sculpture. The human figures now became more symbolic, narrative and moral.

Her earlier work illustrated her concern at the position of woman in relation to her own maleness. Eleanor Jung has said that for women there is a desperate need to recognise their masculine side, because what happens to a woman when the masculine side remains in her subconscious is that it takes over anyway and the woman becomes someone who is always right. Martha sees this reflected in women around her and feels that it is harmful to society. She wishes that women could become aware of their own masculine side and control it, rather than let in remain in the subconscious, repressed to the point where it becomes destructive to children. She feels her grandmother and mother were repressed in this way. They have become dominant matriarchal figures, very male in their behaviour. It is a cumulative thing rather like a snowball, and the daughters lose out all the time. The daughters repress themselves and later on they turn into images of their mothers and there is no way out, it 's like a cage.

Coming back to the present exhibition, she has not only been inspired by the experience of flying and the legend of Icarus, but also reversed the positions and has visually expressed the feminine in the male. The sculptures are strong compositionally and there is less superfluity about them. They are pared back and sophisticated.

Martha makes drawings at the ideas stage, but prefers to work in an intuitive way often finding the forms when working with the material. Her work is very technical, but very well hidden. In her method of slab potting there are great risks: pots can easily twist and crack. She is conscious that one piece in the kiln may be the kiln god, recognition that when she puts a certain piece into the kiln that piece will take care of the others. She is placing things Inside a box again, placing objects into and out of a space. There is a strong sense of integration and heredity about her work.

The 'Young Man' sculpture is of a young militaristic male, stiff with clenched fist, two-breasted and feet firmly on the ground. There is a keyhole shape inside the body and inside this shape is a priestess-like figure who is holding her arms in a spell-weaving way, she is ageless and eternal. There is a softness inside and a hardness on the outside. She has called it 'Young Man' because young men are always trying to be something. The female figure inside controls him, despite him, the space between the solids is a tense space. The keyhole is a narrow-waisted shape, again stressing the feminine figure inside. He has a peculiar type of halo to balance the whole thing because *of so* much weight at the bottom. This gives an iconic feel to the sculpture. He has to have thick legs or else he would physically warp. It is a marriage of symbol, of earthing and practicality. A large figure and a small figure gives importance through scale, but in this case it is reversed. It is white in colour to give the piece more clarity and purity—a coloured glaze would have deadened it.

There is a great deal of ancient Egyptian influence in her work She occasionally looks to *The Book of the Dead* for visual references. Masks from all over the world also play a part, as well as the world of dance, and there is also a theatrical presence in her work.

With 'Icarus,' we see Mother Earth launching the young Icarus. There is a cliff feel to Mother Earth in its profile and boulder-like shape. The two heads are very intent, brows and noses very determined, chins jutting out. The eyes are set back, heads streamlined, everything is pushing. All is concentrated in this business of flight. You almost feel the wind and the way the wind erodes the rock. She has controlled the running of the glaze in 'Icarus' to emphasise a feeling of the horizontal strata of rock. It also reads like a married couple, or a wife pushing her husband into doing something, or a mother pushing her child into doing something.

Martha believes that the human race as a whole tends to have this wish to fly, but needs to be well earthed. She feels that men needed to be reminded of this in 'Icarus' by the Mother Earth figure. In a way, the woman is better earthed than the man.

'Siren' is basically a feminine pregnant bird-like form. The wing/body is also an egg shape and within it there is a small male Icarus. It has a very thick neck, the face flattened like a barn owl or a sun symbol with a strong, cleft chin. A serene face, but it also has a definite smugness about it. She looks pleased with this egg shape because she is saying, "I can do something you cannot!" It is placed, again, on two heavy legs which give it enormous stability. There is a dark side to it:: one could see it as a wife containing her husband.

One can read her work in many different ways. She doesn't want to come to the end of her symbolism. She wants to keep her work enigmatic and exciting, not dogmatic. She has decided she is a deconstructionist.

In the future, it would be good to see her produce work on a larger scale. Her next phase will deal with the relationship between women and between mother and daughter. Some pieces of her work can always be seen at The Salthouse Gallery.

Ray Ambrose

Bob Devereux (September 1986)

Language, when used to describe the work of an artist, can be as dangerous as shot badly loaded in an old blunderbuss, but Ray Ambrose is definitely an explorer, as anyone visiting his exhibition at Falmouth will recognise.

A good retrospective is likely to reveal things about the artist and may provide an opportunity to share his life experience in addition to giving new insights into his paintings.

At 17½ Ray enlisted for military service in India. His regiment was stationed at Jhansi. They were near enough to the jungle to hear the animals roaring at night. When the monsoons came there was a period of intense rain and intense green. The cycle of nature could be clearly sensed at all times. It was this confrontation with a strange landscape which finally decided Ray to paint.

When he was demobbed in 1948, he spent six years in London, painting in odd moments in odd corners. Then he went to Art School, finally being accepted at the Royal Academy school in 1955.

In 1958, Ray went to Spain. It was the music of Manuel de Falla—"The Garden of Spain", heard at a friend's house—which stirred him to go. He spent one month in Madrid making drawings of bullfights and visiting museums and Art Galleries and then, guided by a pin in a map, he went to Muros in Northern Spain, in the Basque region, where he met progressives who were forming an arms syndicate to oppose Franco's regime. Here he painted landscapes full of heat and colour. The reds and ochres of these paintings have mellowed marvellously, like old leather.

On his return to England, he showed at the Young Contemporaries. The British Arts Council selected his work, with the work of 24 others, to tour Britain. One of the paintings from that show will be in the exhibition—"The Yellow Room". Although it is an interior painted in England it reflects the colour and the feeling of his earlier Spanish paintings.

The more one discovers, the greater the mystery. Ray has always been a lover of poetry, for its music and its layered imagery. He came across a book of Dylan Thomas' collected works in a secondhand bookshop in 1961. One poem in particular, "The Winter's Tale," grew in his imagination until it became imperative to visualise the experience. The influence of Blake and Chagall can be clearly seen not only in the paintings, but in the spinning imagery of Thomas' words. In the truest sense these can be called spiritual paintings and it is at this point that I would be tempted to recognise Ray as a symbolist.

Throughout the late 1960s and the early 1970s Ray was moved to paint the sea; searching out its rhythms and abstracting its moods. Then, in 1975, he became interested in astronomy, and would go out with a friend at two in the morning to watch the display of the universe through a telescope at Tredarvoe. The ghostly, spiralling gulls and the magnificent vista of the heavens became the subject of his next paintings—a fusion of imagination and experience; recollections of that other great sky over India. In some of the bird forms, there is an acknowledgement of Braque and the bird he uses in his studio paintings.

A visit to Brittany, touring along the coast with a friend in 1983, led to another series of land-and seascapes and several of these very spontaneous paintings will also be in the show.

Ray has been interested in Jazz since the age of 11. He's recently picked up his clarinet again and is sitting in with various groups around the county. This revived interest in music has led to a group of paintings which I think are the strongest he has yet produced. Large figure compositions of his family, the Jazz bands and of a sextet being rehearsed by a lady composer with whom he's become friendly. These seem to be packed with so much emotion and richness of experience that they are well worth the journey he has made to arrive at them. The large painting, "My Life", in which Ray, looking not unlike the god Pan, plays his clarinet whilst the family chaos rages around him expressed all of the claustrophobia of a marriage fraught with difficulties with great pathos and true humour.

Wilhelmina Barns-Graham

Annette Robinson
(July 1989)

The recent retrospective exhibition at the Newlyn Gallery of Wilhelmina Barns-Graham's paintings presented much more than 50 years of her work: it exposed a very personal world, a lifelong relationship between artist and subject, a love affair with the very fabric of West Penwith. St Ives is her home of many years, and the growth and development of the modern art movement is recorded in her work with masterly strokes.

Wilhelmina Barns-Graham came to St Ives in 1940. She was born in St Andrews, Scotland, in 1912 and studied at the Edinburgh College of Art from 1932-37. During that time she was awarded several scholarships, and visited Paris, Rouen and San Tropez, studying and working as she travelled. She was impressed by the work of Vermeer, Courbet, Turner, Piero Della Francesca and Cezanne.

It was not her wish to settle in Cornwall. She suffered ill-health and it was on the advice of her tutor, Hubert Wellington, that she arrived in St Ives on a year's travelling scholarship. He considered that the environment would be good for her health and that she would be in sympathy with artists already working here, artists such as Ben Nicholson, Naum and Miriam Gabo and Margaret Mellis, with whom she had studied and travelled.

It was not even love at first sight. After six months, Barns-Graham reported back that she was not happy in St Ives, but after her year was up she did not leave. By 1942 she had put down roots and became a member of both the Newlyn Society and St Ives Society of Artists.

She lived and worked in the intensely creative environment of St Ives in the '40s and '50s, when the foundations were being laid for the establishment of the modern art movement. It was Barns-Graham who was instrumental in 1943, along with friend and artist Borlaze Smart, in getting the 'moderns' into the St Ives Society.

It wasn't easy, and the group were never really allowed to integrate. They became known as the 'artists around the font' as they were limited to a small exhibition space near the main doors of the society's converted mariners' chapel.

Barns-Graham's work at this time was still mainly descriptive, but an underlying abstract structure was growing, in tune with other resident artists such as Peter Lanyon, Sven Berlin, Bryan Wynter, John Wells and Guido Morris. Together they were struggling for recognition in an area ruled by academic, figurative art.

The Castle Inn in Fore Street was their meeting place. Landlord Endell Mitchell was a keen supporter of their work and paintings that are now the treasures of art collectors and large institutions all over the world were hung on the walls of his bar. Over drinks, ideas were exchanged, plans were made and artist supported artist through times of hardship.

In 1949, Barns-Graham, along with 16 other modern and figurative artists, resigned from the St Ives Society of Artists. As a direct result, the Penwith Society of Artists was founded at a meeting at the Castle Inn. Barns-Graham was a founder member and still contributes work to the present day.

Throughout the 1950s the avant-garde style of this small group flourished and through them St Ives became a world-recognised centre for modern art. Barns-Graham's work represents these years with great charm, even through periods of personal upheaval

Her *Red Painting* of 1957 painted at the end of her marriage to writer David Lewis, is angry and fiercely defiant. By this time her work was bold and confident. She travelled to France, Italy and Spain, always bringing back fresh ideas and inspiration from visits to other European artists or collectors, such as Peggy Guggenheim, whom she visited in Venice in 1954.

In 1960, she inherited a house in St Andrews and since then has split her time between Scotland and Cornwall. This renewed her ties with Edinburgh, and it was from there that her retrospective exhibition was launched.

Her heart is still in St Ives, where she spends as much time as she can. She feels that her current work has an urgency "a desperation to say it now." Her latest paintings in gouache and acrylic are certainly more free and expressive, proof that the adventure of art goes on forever.

Max Barrett

Martin Val Baker (June 1985)

Over the last few years one of the most interesting new artists to show in the local galleries has been the wood carver and sculptor Max Barrett. Max lives in a secluded caravan In Carbis Bay surrounded by a mass of striking images in wood and stone and it was here that the *Voice* talked to him.

Unusually for his particular line of work, Max Barrett is in fact Cornish (born in Penzance in 1937) and so is one of that thin band of native artists who include Bryan Pearce, Dick Gilbert, Margo Maekelberge, Jack Pender and, of course, the late Peter Lanyon. In his teens Max worked on local farms, driving a horse and cart and doing all the many odd jobs that farming entails—although the work was hard he enjoyed it and learnt very much to appreciate the seasons and the effect they have on the countryside. During his three year's national service he was trained as an engineer and rigger and later worked in the steel industry all over the country eventually settling in Southampton.

Twelve years ago Max decided the time had come to return to Cornwall and he left Southampton with the intention of trying his hand at painting—despite having had no formal training. He had been impressed by a tall ships race at Southampton and took these magnificent beasts as his first subjects, feeling though that their beauty was only skin deep. On his return, Max swapped his car for an old furniture lorry and lived in this for over a year in various car parks and lay-bys around Penwith; the lorry doubled as a makeshift studio and also as storage space for the scrap metal from which he made his living at the time. ('Quite a good living too.') Eventually Max became frustrated by the limitations of paint as a medium, 'Painting can't get behind, above and over the subject' and soon after losing his toe, began 'whittling' and carving images in bits of found wood.

In 1975 he had a bit of luck when he was able to buy three tons of wood from the estate of Barbara Hepworth, 'beautiful wood, Irish yew and gurnia from Africa.' The Wills Lane Gallery was the first to exhibit his carvings (previously he sold them in pubs) and gallery owner Mr Gilbert soon suggested that he should try the local Delabole slate as a medium, one that took Max over a year to conquer but is now his favourite material. 'The hardest thing I've worked, it's like the leaves of a book and very easy to go wrong with.' Max particularly likes the effect of water on slate but finds that waxing it tends to make the slate too dark and metallic. He has experimented with many different waxes but now feels confident that the slate can stand on its own without an artificial skin. (Incidentally he is much against stands or frames).

Max likes to emphasise the natural patterns of both wood and slate, 'It's like a dance where you don't dictate the moves but the material takes the lead—but if you lose concentration it's gone.' The tougher pieces of wood, full of knots are harder to work but much more satisfying in the end—'Like a book that can be picked up and read again and again.

The availability of materials decides the size of any particular piece, and the smaller works are often more difficult than the larger ones. Max feels that although city people seem to be in the forefront of art movements you are either 'city wise or country wise' and that 'the truth is out there in the country.'

As well as slate Max also works with rustic stone and driftwood (an 8ft high shag, in driftwood, adorns his garden); and used two seabeaten stanchions from the old collapsed quay behind Smeatons at St Ives, 'Can't understand how Berlin and Hepworth missed 'em!' Max's famous 'Gentle Wave' commissioned by the St Ives Festival in 1982 and now resting at Land's End 'will take ten years to work.' The sculptor was a little upset when the piece was covered with canvas one winter 'the weather should erode it like the land around it.' He got the cover removed.

I asked Max about other artists and he said that he would put Sven Berlin above Hepworth, 'a brave man,' and finds the latter 'cerebral rather than instinctive.' Denis Mitchel and Paul Mount also have a sense of individualism. Of the painters he admires Kate Nicholson above all others, 'very powerful,' John Wells, Bob Bourne and of the younger generation, Richard Ayling and Victoria Burlton as well as David Kemp's creations. Max is violently against committees, groups and other such organisations, feeling that they 'promote mediocrity,' and very much for the individualists who have the courage of their convictions.

As he pushed my car down the lane, Max called out 'Don't go making me seem too arrogant.'

Pete Berryman

Martin Val Baker (December 1988)

Pete Berryman was born and bred in Newquay. His early musical influences were the records of Presley, Holly, Steele and the Everleys. Moving to boarding school in Launceston he met up with another well-known Cornish guitar player Spike Hooper (now of the Flying Tigers), who taught him his first chords on the guitar. It was, in fact, with Spike's group 'The Launceston College Jazz Band' that Pete made his first public performance. "We had one jazz number, the rest were things like *I Go Ape*. We used to play a rock 'n roll set in the interval at the local Ceildh. I played drums but moved to guitar as soon as possible."

After leaving school, Pete played with a number of semi-pro Cornish rock 'n roll bands. "We went through every style from early Shadows stuff (we used to wear the suits and do all the steps), to the Beatles and the Rolling Stones."

At one time, the nineteen-year-old Berryman and a friend moved to London to 'make it,' recording a single for EMI at the famous Abbey Road studios, though this venture soon failed due to 'terrible management.'

Although he was aware of the folk boom, Pete was not really interested until by chance he saw a TV programme, *Hullabaloo* featuring amongst others the legendary guitarist Davey Graham ... "He really blew my mind!" Like many of his contemporaries, Pete learned Davey Graham's classic guitar instrumental *Angie*—"but not note for note—I did my own version and I still play it; I did it on Saturday night."

Now playing acoustic guitar, he began to travel a bit, though "I was no good at busking; I was too shy." In London, Pete joined folk group THE HAVERING as a bass player! "I conned them into letting me play and then went out and bought a beaten up double bass." With THE HAVERING, Pete toured the country for six months playing "Jewish songs, music hall and some contemporary stuff."

Following the demise of the group, Pete returned to Newquay, where local banjo player Barney Potter persuaded him to pay a visit to the thriving Folk Cottage Club at nearby Mitchell.

The Folk Cottage at that time had a 'house band' which featured Ralph McTell, Whispering Mick Bennet, Henry the Jug and Bob Strawbridge and soon Pete Berryman, too, was a regular member. THE FAMOUS JUG BAND, as it became, went through various personnel changes, eventually emerging as a quartet with Pete on guitar, Henry on jug, and the newly arrived Clive Palmer on banjo, whilst Jill Johnson was responsible for the vocals.

The FJB quickly established a reputation and a string of folk club bookings throughout the country followed. Guitarist Wizz Jones, who had just recorded an LP for United Artists, recommended the band to his producer Pierre Tubbs, and in 1969 *Sunshine Possibilities* was released. This album, featuring songs by Pete and Clive, as well as original arrangements of traditional numbers, became a classic of that era, one of the highlights being Pete's high sensitive guitar work on *A Leaf Must Fall*. The follow-up record, *Chameleon*, was not such a success and with hindsight Pete feels that he indulged himself a little after Clive Palmer's departure and that there should have been inputs from other directions.

Pete has fond memories of those days, when the FJB was resident at the old Railway (now the Longboat) club in Penzance in the company of the JAZZ ROOTS, THE TEMPLE CREATURES, MIKE SILVER *et al.* Temporary members of the band at that time included both Wizz Jones and John James (with whom Pete was later to record another folk classic *Sky in my Pie*).

After a spell on the continent, Pete returned to England and teamed up with Al Schmitt and Dick Cadbury as TOTEM for a while. Then an extraordinary opportunity presented itself: the American band MORMOS had come to Europe as backing group for La Mama Theatre Company and stayed on in Paris when the parent company returned home. In France they had become very popular and released a couple of LPs. Of all places, they had ended up in Camelford and it was there that Pete Berryman joined them on guitar as they prepared for a (pre-Womad) tour of Africa. MORMOS operated on the borders of theatre, jazz and rock with a lot of humour and a line-up that included sax, flute, guitar, cello, vocals and percussion. The tour of Liberia, the Ivory Coast and Algeria, is described by Pete as "an incredible experience," although at one time there was nearly a riot when a group of Algerians suspected the group of being American propagandists!

"We were just a bunch of spaced out hippies." No more sleeping on floors though; the group stayed in hotels, drank with diplomats at cocktail parties and even met the Liberian cabinet at one stage

Music in Africa was very western-influenced at that time; it seemed that all the local bands played *Green, Green Grass of Home* and James Brown was a big influence. Hearing the advice in Algeria that 'no drums means no music' Mormos took the precaution of hiring local drummers at each of their gigs.

Returning to Paris, Pete teamed up with another ex-Mormos musician, cellist Sandy Spencer and, with Michael Hanks, toured Britain as SADIE later turning up solo on *The Old Grey Whistle Test* ... "Terrible—one of my most embarrassing moments."

Recording opportunities came, with guest appearances on albums by Ralph McTell and Wizz Jones and Pete later toured Europe with a wonderfully anarchic internationally flavoured band called NOAH'S ROADSHOW. "We were absolutely skint, but didn't quite starve."

Back in England, Pete next joined American Thom Pedgeresky as musical backing for the French clown Daniel Rovai and his German partner Margaritte Biereye in their enormously talented *Barney's Pocket Show*, an offshoot of Footsbarn and perhaps the greatest theatrical and musical experience to emerge from Cornwall. The Barneys toured Europe to delighted audiences and the money was good, too!

For something completely different, Pete got a job as accompanist to singer Julix Felix, touring Australia and New Zealand as well as playing at one of the famous Hyde Park Free Concerts. Whilst in the Pacific, Pete took the opportunity to join the Anti-Nuclear boat *Fri* for a while, sailing in her to the New Hebrides.

Back in Europe, Pete recorded a solo LP in Germany and one in Holland: "Funky chamber music with guitar, cello, violin and flute, but it was indefinable and difficult to market and so was not released." Stefan Grossman, of KICKING MULE

Nowadays, Pete works as a guitar teacher. As a free-lance musician he plays with C&W bands and with rock groups. He writes music for theatre groups: "Doing what's required for all situations." He knows that there are very few outlets for the music closest to his heart—acoustic guitar music really needs a concert stage. However, with the exciting BLUE TICKET it is a little easier as the group crosses the border between being a listening band and playing in pubs and getting away with it.

Bob Bourne

Mike Venning (July 1986)

Bob Bourne's pictures aren't immediate, they're not spectacular nor flashy, but have a slow-burning inner strength. The more you look, the more you feel: They have a capacity to move the onlooker through their honesty and the way that they cut right through superficiality and head directly for the depths of human relationships. Bob paints his way into areas few artists dare enter and succeeds in capturing the tensions that invade humans in their attempts to relate to each other.

Painting, particularly figurative work, is a curious method of expression: a mix of colours in a combination of shapes that satisfies aesthetic requirements and yet provides comment or insight into the human condition. Why should certain mixes of shape and colour have so much more meaning than other equally aesthetically pleasant groupings? For Bob, the answer is in the overtones that remain with the spectator once the painting has been seen and left. Good painting has meaning beyond the confines of the canvas. This is a quality certainly evident in his work. He also believes that a painting has a life of its own when finished. The communication between the artist and his work has ended, now it's up to the people who look at it.

Thus art works operate as an interface between the imagination of the artist and that of the spectator. Quite so with Bob Bourne's paintings, the characters are his, the colours and interpretation of landscape are his, but they provide fuel for the onlooker's mind. Likewise the feelings expressed in Bob's paintings are his own, but we can recognise them instantly, they are common to us all. Most often they seem to be those paradoxical emotions which constantly occur in situations where humans get close to one another. One notes, and feels, the tension that accompanies love, the sadness hiding beneath the surface of happy activity, even the quirky fun that is lurking in a sombre face. Landscape can provide a sense of space and freedom, or equally feel claustrophobic.

The paintings do communicate, one's thoughts and feelings are stirred, yet these constitute interpretations, valid in themselves, but not necessarily in accord with Bob's view of his work. Here lies a basic difficulty in writing about such paintings. They are not exercises in technical skill, nor polemic *tours de force* which invite comment and speculation due to their qualitative nature. On the contrary, they capture the fleeting and non-quantifiable nuances of human interaction. This is even apparent in the landscapes which always contain evidence of human existence (inevitable, the only way to miss it is to look out to sea, and hope you see no ships). Each landscape is also stamped with Bob's feelings. They are not just representations of what is there to be seen, but are the result of long-term work in the studio, subject to the fluctuations of the artist's moods during this period.

Turning to the technical side of things, colour is important, Bob uses thin glazes of paint to attain subtlety both in the interaction of colour over the surface of the painting and in its depth. Sometimes he makes vivid contrasts, sometimes muted tones are carefully blended. Bob's drawing may look naive but is far from it. Figures are considered critically and fitted into the overall composition with precision. The process is a sophisticated one, not the spontaneous expression of naiveté. He uses a deceptively limpid line, which risks being flaccid but never is, in fact it adds further sensitivity to the pictures.

All this is subservient to the picture working: he may persevere with a painting for years before he feels that it's right. A picture will be pared down until it's balanced and there are no loose ends in either aesthetic or subject terms. What counts is that this combination of skill, thought and emotion works for Bob, then the struggle to blend those disparate elements is over and painting and artist part company.

Bob Bourne has worked long and hard to produce a body of remarkable paintings. Influences have appeared fleetingly and have been discarded, the path Bob follows is very much his own. The pictures that demonstrate this far better than any words will be exhibited at the Penwith Gallery, St. Ives, from 12 July to 2 August, in combination with carvings by Max Barrett.

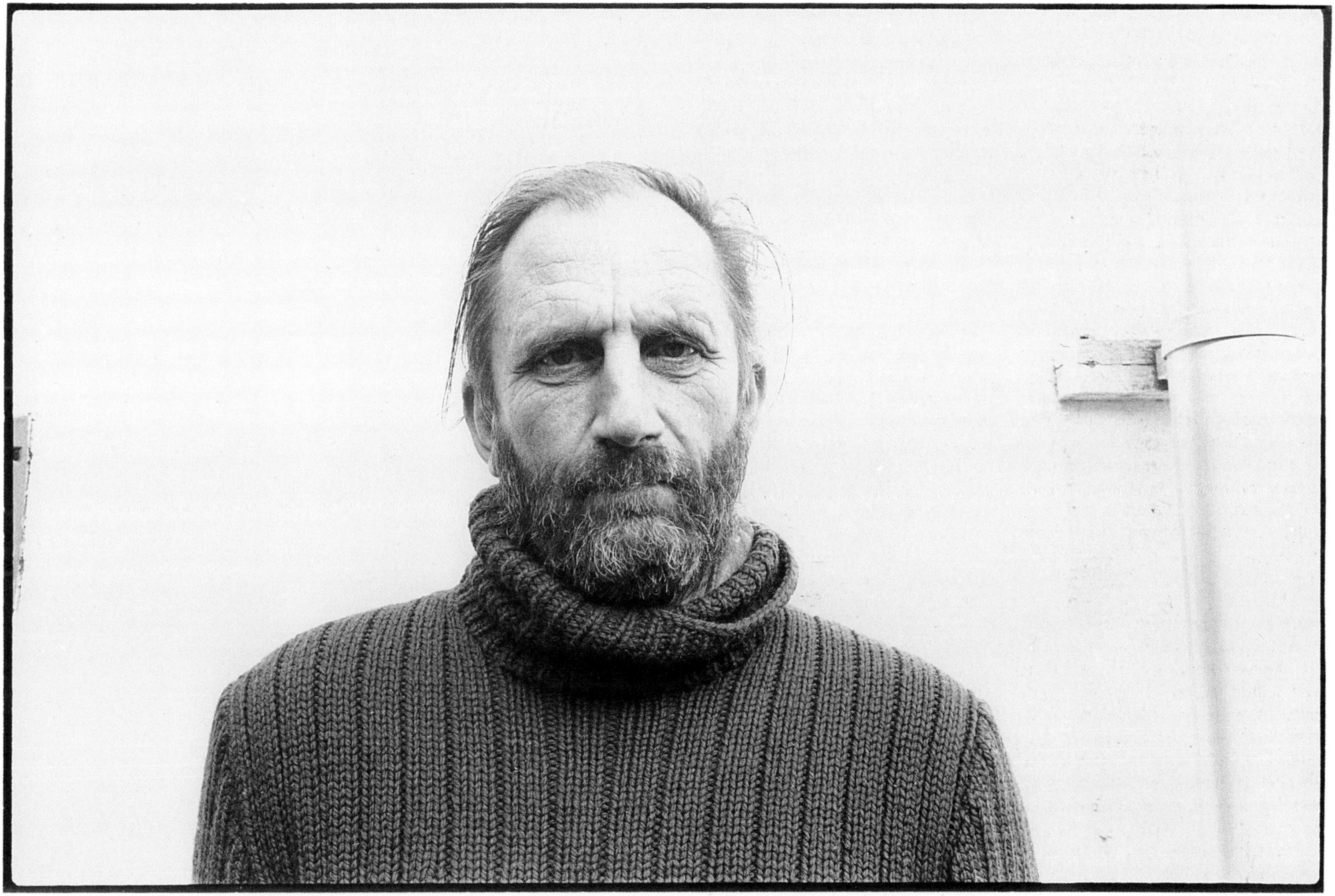

Roger Brooks

Martin Val Baker (April 1985)

Since the collapse of the seventies' Folk boom and the consequent closing down of the major part of the country's folk club circuit, many British performers have been forced to travel abroad in search of work. Indeed, a number of fairly well known artists have been forced to give up completely and find a new career after twenty years as professional entertainers. One who has so far stayed the course and earned his living exclusively as a performer is the St Ives based singer/songwriter Roger Brooks, who left last week for a month's work in Scandinavia.

Roger first came to St Ives from Nottingham in 1970 as a rather flashy guitarist in the Graham/Jansch/Renbourn mould and played regularly at the Mask Club. After leaving university, he served the long apprenticeship of floor spots, residencies and constant travel throughout the country, gradually developing an extrovert stage presence to sell his act. By the mid-seventies he had become an accomplished songwriter, whose work was being covered by many of his contemporaries, and was getting regular bookings as guest artist on the circuit. In 1975, Brooks travelled to New York performing at colleges and on radio shows and then, after a spell in Paris, returned to Britain for extensive tours over the next few years. Regular appearances on Capital Radio with Richard Digance, and a growing following, indicated a promising future for Brooks, but Britain's folk boom was beginning to peter out.

In 1980, contact with a Dutch agent opened up a new avenue, and a long series of one-nighters in Holland and Germany brought Brooks much hard work and also enabled him to get a flat in St Ives to use as a permanent base. The same year a London agent arranged some bookings in Norway and he has returned to do a month-long stint there twice annually ever since. Besides his European ventures, Roger still tours the surviving English clubs and is particularly popular in the Midlands (where he has a group of fans called the Leaking Whippets!) and the south coast.

In the summer, Roger performs locally as a pub act, either solo or as a duo with guitarist Don Fowler from Carbis Bay (Local Heroes) usually working six nights a week. At the pub and hotel gigs Roger rarely performs his own songs as he has learned from experience that these audiences want familiar commercial numbers as a background to a social night out, and that it is only when an admission fee has been paid, will he have a properly attentive audience.

At one time Roger Brooks seemed destined for the 'Big Time'; his songs were the equal of many, more 'successful' writers, but perhaps he was born a few years too late. As more and more commercial work is necessitated and opportunities to perform his work decline, the sharp edges get smoothed out. Ambitious as ever, he intends to move to London next winter to concentrate on the city venues and record another album: a survivor who has lived entirely by his music for twelve years.

Alan Brough

Martin Green (February 1988)

Not all men are lucky enough to have a vocation in life, and of those that do, not all of them are able to marry that vocation with the means by which they gain their livelihood. One such is Alan Brough, of the pottery in Duke Street, Newlyn, across the carpark from the back of the Co-op. Alan is an upright, white-bearded humorist who discovered a long time ago that life without laughter is not worth a light. He claims there is a touch of Viking in his blood, as well as a touch of French, and his father's research into the family name found a meaning in it, 'leader of a hundred'. His research stopped there, when he had to ask himself, the leader of a hundred what? His was a family of makers and doers, his father being a sculptor and another relative being involved with the famous 'Superior' motorcycle associated with his name.

Alan Brough was born near Wilmslow, Cheshire, just long enough ago to get himself caught up in World War II, and he served in a navy that was still redolent, in Winston Churchill's phrase, of "rum, buggery and the lash'. While he was happy to fight in a war to destroy Hitler, and all that fascism stood for, he'd had enough of war itself when he came out and it was this as much as anything else that decided him on becoming a potter, that he would be a maker of things rather than a destroyer.

He went to the Camberwell School of Art, then a lively place fertilised by the artistic excitement of the time, when painters such as Rodrigo Moynihan, John Minton, Keith Vaughan, Robert MacBryde, Robert Colquhoun, John Caxton and Leonard Rosoman, could be met both as teachers and practising artists.

These artists, and their work at that time, have been dismissed latterly as 'romantic' by the art world journalists, but all of them were artists with the true prophetic vision which is instantly recognisable whenever their work is encountered afresh. If the English were less Philistine there would be a gallery, or a number of rooms in a gallery somewhere, devoted to the work of these 'romantics'. It is difficult now to recall that heady post-war delight simply in creation, for it is not something encountered in the art schools of today.

From art school, Alan Brough set up in London as a potter, supplying a demand for attractive pottery to people wanting something more than the utility-ware they had forced upon them immediately after the war, but the business ceased to be viable as soon as the restrictions on imported pottery were lifted in the early Fifties and cheap pottery flooded in from abroad.

Alan came westwards to Devon and for a time worked in the Dartmouth pottery making purely commercial, mass-produced work. This, however, became too much for a man whose own creative resources weren't being tapped, and with a mental crisis looming, he asked his spiritual guide and mentor, Bernard Leach, if he would take him on at his pottery in St Ives. Leach agreed, and employed him on a basic wage, also providing accommodation, and Alan was able to resolve the problems that had been looming up in his head.

It was some fifteen years ago that he took over the pottery at Newlyn, which had been in the possession of the son of the director of the Newlyn Gallery, McCleod, and it was here that he found the true marriage between his calling and the bread-and-butter needed for him to exercise it. His wife Sheila, a dressmaker, shares the premises and works upstairs.

One of the striking things about Alan's work is its immediacy and unpretentiousness. You don't feel, as you do with some of the work of Leach, or other exalted potters, that when you are handling something, you are lifting up a philosophical or artistic concept, but that you are lifting up an honest piece of pottery. That it is pleasing to the eye and the senses generally is as it should be. The spirit of John Ruskin would find peace in Alan Brough's pottery, for it was Ruskin who said, among many other memorable things about the work of man, that "fine art is that in which the hand, the head, and the heart of man go together".

I have always taken exception to Dr Johnson's remark that no man is more harmlessly employed than when he is making money, for I have worked for people whose sole aim was making money, and it is a cancer. But I would happily go along with the assertion re-phrased, that no man is more harmlessly employed than when he is making something himself which will make him a living. The word 'maker' in Greek is the same as the word for poet, and Alan Brough is a maker all right, a maker of honest and beautiful pottery.

At the end of November and into December, his work is to be exhibited at Balliol College, Oxford, alongside the work of another local artist, Olivia Steadman.

With the season of Christmas approaching, you'd do better for your family and friends in Alan's pottery than in a thousand tawdry high street shops. As the man said, a thing of beauty is a joy forever.

Anthony Bryant

Mike Venning (November 1988)

Anthony Bryant was born in West Cornwall, an area of the country .lacking in trees, which might seem to be an impediment to someone whose life has become intimately connected with wood and with a particular need for variety of mature timber. However, circumstances were beneficial and Anthony, as the son of a carpenter and builder, got to know about wood and what you could do with it during his childhood. He even got to practise on an old treadle lathe, and, like any inventive teenager, turned out a variety of objects.

On the surface nothing stirred: OK you're having fun, but is it going to earn you a living? What do you do when you don't know what to do? Anthony became a bank clerk.

The seeds had been sown, however, but germination was a while coming. A catalyst was required, and one came along clad in the most innocent disguise. Bored stiff in the bank, Anthony was desperately looking for some kind of holiday that would transport him out of the world of balance sheets, grey suits and ties. He noticed an advert for wood-turning courses, thought why not (maybe a chord was struck), and went. The course in question was run by Mike Law, an industrial woodturner living at Maxworthy in the deepest wilds of North Cornwall.

A holiday messing around with wood turned Anthony's life on its head. Mike Law was the key that opened the lock on his imagination and, as he experimented both under Mike's guidance and on his own, so his love for wood was confirmed, along with the realisation that this was the medium in which his self-expression could flower.

Still working in the bank, he dedicated his weekends and evenings to woodturning, trying out techniques and finding out more about wood. Characteristically, even while indulging in turning as a pastime, Anthony was making decisions about his future direction. He discovered that he preferred working with green wood—fresh wood, still full of sap unlike the dried and relatively inert substance most often used by woodworkers. While working with green wood is a more risky business than working with seasoned timber, especially for the novice, it is a measure of Anthony's determination and self-confidence that he took this course, and, with the additional help of hard work, has had spectacular success.

The pace at which Anthony was assimilating expertise and the gathering intensity of his involvement in woodturning called for a choice between banking and craftwork to be made. The turning point perhaps? This was no contest. Whatever the risks, a career in banking was cast aside and Anthony took the plunge into full-time woodturning. A romantic move? Maybe, but he had his eyes open, and it was a considered decision to put all of his energy where his heart was.

In no way is Anthony Bryant half-hearted. If banking had been his desire, he would have a successful career in that sphere by now. He has never had any illusions about the hard work involved in making one's way as a craftsman; in objective terms the world of banking would have been the soft option.

It was no holds barred once Anthony started woodturning full-time. As mentioned already, he wasn't prepared to play safe and, while he obviously didn't reach his goals immediately, he was moving determinedly in his own direction. Progress in art and craft is achieved by overcoming self-set problems; you have a feel for something and then it's a case of negotiating the obstacles. While craftwork can be considered as an attainment of particular skills, in Anthony's case he had to make his skills match his vision. Not a practice-makes-perfect situation: vision is a moving target for artist, craftsman or writer, imagination always stays one step ahead of the hands and the best piece of work is the one to come

Firstly, green wood sounds like an obstacle that skill would overcome. Maybe so on one level—you become used to the material and its quirks and make progress. However, the wood has a life of its own. The craftsman has done his work, but the wood may warp and twist, it may even split. Anthony has therefore developed his vision to go with the idiosyncrasies of the material, at first by cutting and reworking bowls so that design obliterated the wood's waywardness. This proved unsatisfactory; the bowls were good but had a slightly stilted air. He was still fighting the nature of the material, looking too much to put his design onto the wood rather than draw it out.

The second challenge was to turn bowls to a remarkably delicate degree of thinness, not a task to be taken lightly when you're gouging into a large piece of fast-spinning wood with a razor-sharp chisel. Technically difficult though it is, Anthony feels that certain woods need this delicacy of treatment in order to accentuate their grain and markings. Outstanding examples are the bowls he made out of pale figured sycamore whose semi-transparent fragility brings out the full beauty of the wood's silky markings. less, his technical skills should not be underestimated, for the sureness of outstanding.

The two particular areas of woodturning to which Anthony has applied himself reflect his basic love of its properties, oddities, patterns and marks that only comes from closeness to and respect for the material. He enjoys the whole process of his occupation, from the felling and cutting up of each tree, which most often happens on chillingly cold or wet and windy days in late autumn or winter, through the transformation from raw wood to finished artefact.

Work of the quality that Anthony is producing deserves recognition, and in the last couple of years this has occurred in almost exponential proportions. He received a Crafts Council grant in 1986, then exhibited at the Chelsea Crafts Fair, which really seemed to put his name on the map. Next came an invitation to show at the New York International Gift Fair in 1987, returning this year, and now he is much in demand in the United States. He has shows coming in Los Angeles and Connecticut, while interest is blossoming in Japan. Meanwhile, Anthony's work can be found in many places in Britain, and nowhere more impressively than in the present Craftwork Show at the Newlyn Orion.

The work on show at Newlyn this month is a good representation of Anthony's recent output. They are all large pieces and are exhilarating in their mix of daring expertise and the sheer beauty and grace that emanates; from the wood.

The wood's warping after the work has been finished creates shapes beyond the compass of human hand and eye, the burr wood whirls and clots, mis-shapen but superb, none of which would have been visible but for the skill and understanding of Anthony Bryant.

The vessels here seem closer to sculpture than utilitarian artefacts. Each is unique and the result of Anthony's uncanny ability to read the pattern of markings in a lump of wood and turn a bowl whose shape fits the wood's figures perfectly. The future's a fascinating thought: Anthony's not out ot his twenties yet, and his achievement so far would indicate that there's a lot more to come.

Victoria Burlton

Annette Robinson (August 1985)

Victoria Burlton's exhibition showing throughout July has attracted much interest from visitors to the Salthouse Gallery. Her paintings are full of movement, sometimes obvious, sometimes obscure, but each one interesting enough to demand a closer look.

She completed a foundation course at Exeter Art College, and from 1974/77 attended Ravensbourne Art School. She studied sculpture, but by the time she had finished the course she had decided to take up painting instead. Colour is very important to her, but when she tried to introduce colours into her sculpture at college her efforts were not met with approval.

In 1978 she moved to Cornwall. She spent her first winter in the relative luxury of a winter let at Acton Castle, then spent the next five years in two caravans on Rosudgeon Common, Living in one and painting in the other. She decided to leave the Common before the final fight against eviction orders that have befallen the unfortunate remaining residents. Now she lives in a house in St Just, working in a garden shed until something more suitable can be built.

Her work looks very much at home on the walls of the Salthouse Gallery, and Bob and Jenny Devereux are showing faith in what they see, rather than awaiting the approval of the "reputation makers" of the art world The exhibition speaks for itself.

The New Craftsman Gallery in Fore Street, St Ives, has a number of her paintings permanently installed among their abundant selection of work, either on display or available for perusal

In 1982 she exhibited in the Montmartre district of Paris. Impressed with the quality of work she saw there, Victoria Burlton took the short step from Dover and staged a small but successful exhibition.

Her efforts in this country, however, have hit a wall of attitude that seems to prevail—"Come back when we know your name." It is fortunate for Victoria Burlton, and others in the same situation trying to gain a reputation, that not all doors are closed to them.

Bob Butler

Martin Val Baker (December 1986)

Bob's introduction to the unpredictable but addictive world of showbiz was in 1976, when he and some friends organised a series of monthly village hall gigs at St. Ewe just outside Mevagissey. The success of these promotions eventually led to the founding of a summer festival at nearby Polgooth which ran for three summers up to 1979. From the start the organising committee sought local support and every household within two miles of the site was given an explanatory leaflet and the goodwill obtained from local residents helped balance the police attitude which Bob felt "was negative from the start; they didn't make any effort whatsoever to understand what we were doing or why we were doing it.". Polgooth Fayre grew in popularity each year, featuring the best Cornish acts and introducing new and unfamiliar acts to the county, such as: Forkbeard Fantasy, The Lemmings, Tosh, Ekome Dance, Kevin Coyne, Zoot Money, 5 hand reel, The Greatest Show on Legs and many more. However, in 1979 the Fayre attracted the unwelcome attentions of the early Peace Convoy, and whilst Bob felt that the organisers managed to cope with the Convoy, the added hassle of an antagonistic local police presence eventually brought the Fayre to an end. In fact Bob spent most of the final day at St. Austell persuading the police not to close down the Fayre and enrage a crowd of 10,000. Bob still has fond memories of a jam session that year with old 'stringbander' Robin Williamson, local resident Ralph McTell and Fairport's Dave Pegg.

After a year off, Bob once again began to get the itch for the world of festivals, and it was at the 1980 Festival of Fools in Penzance that he and a friend conceived the idea of what was to become Elephant Fayre. Whilst they were searching for a site, someone suggested that they should contact a reclusive aristocrat who lived at St. Germans, Lord Eliot, who owned a superb estate around his ancestral home Port Eliot. Perry Eliot had been involved in showbiz years before as a merchandiser of Beatles paraphernalia, and he reacted to Bob's ideas with enthusiasm. Once again local people were leafleted (and given free tickets to the Fayre) and this, (plus feudal ties with the Eliot family!) ensured local support. Bob's job in the collective who ran Elephant Fayre was to book most of the artistes and his finely tuned sense of feel in this field ensured the arrival of some remarkable acts in Cornwall. With hindsight, Bob feels that the booking of Siouxsle and the Banshees and other cult bands, though a huge success, acquired the Fayre the reputation as a Rock venue to the detriment of other less popular Art forms. Balancing the programme in fact is a vital skill and Elephant Fayre was noted for strong bookings in the fields of Reggae, Theatre, Cabaret, Folk, Poetry and experimental arts as well as the rock acts necessary to guarantee the large audiences. It was in the public's interest to have a high turnover of acts and this often meant turning down re-bookings, particularly local performers, although, as Bob says, the Fayre gave a platform for "every half-way decent local act." After four years intensive work on Elephant, Bob felt the need for a change, "there is only a certain length of time you can spend dealing with rock agents—they're the lowest form of life" and he felt drawn to a less hectic life. For a year Bob edited a new Plymouth magazine *Barker* and then, after dabbling at independent cabaret and folk promotions, he turned to the theatre.

Knee High. Theatre had been started in 1979 and Bob had been friendly with them from the beginning, often booking them at Elephant. In July, 1985, an opportunity arose to become the professional administrator with the group and Bob took the plunge. Coming from a background of commercial entertainment, he had to take a crash course in the precarious ways of theatrical existence and the mysteries of state funding of the arts. Knee High had previously got project grants for their productions *Jungle Book* and *The Three Musketeers* and gradually funding from South West Arts and the National Arts Council has been improving. With eleven full-time and nine part-time employees the compan,y needs to generate £100,000 a year, and they could not get that in takings, at least not without leaving Cornwall, where there are only three venues capable of paying a straight fee.

Thinking of the lamented exit of the under-funded Footsbarn in 1979, I asked Bob Butler if Knee High would also eventually move out of the county, but he strenuously denied this, "Footsbarn were a truly itinerant company whilst Knee High have strong local roots.". "Wouldn't it help to be more centrally based?" I asked, thinking this time of Orchard Theatre, but Bob feels that Orchard's massive funding has more to do with "historic and political reasons rather than where they are based or the quality of their work." Speculation on Orchard's possible loss of grant continues and after eight years such a move would be crippling for the company, though as Bob says, the decision not to fund other companies properly is just as crippling in itself. Bob himself would like to see the S.W.A.Theatre Grant (of which Orchard takes 60%—£110,000) redistributed more evenly, but feels that the organisation will not confront the central problem—what will happen to Orchard if their funding is drastically reduced. Knee High, Dr Fosters and several other companies in the South West have demonstrated that there would not be a vacuum. The National Arts Council reports that it gets more applications from Theatre Groups in the south west than any other region, the reason being that no other regional Arts Association invests so much of its budget in one company.

As tor Knee High themselves, Bob feels that "around £30,000" in today's terms is the maximum funding they could accept without affecting the ambitions of other companies in the area, but he realises that S.W.A. are hamstrung by shortage of money, and Cornwall C.C.'s consistent low funding of the Arts does not help matters (£30,000 as opposed to Devon's £200,000). With the recent formation of a Knee High Theatre Schools Group which gives the company more depth, Bob feels that they can fulfill their aim of "producing shows that people can come to and not be offended or have to listen to political diatribes, always working with new material, innovative directors and original writers."

Norman Stuart Clarke

Pam Otto (October 1985)

Norman Stuart Clarke is an engaging and energetic cockney, who at his home in Praze-an-Beeble makes some of the most beautiful free blown studio glass to be found today. It is most unfortunate that we are unable to reproduce his work in colour because it's the gorgeous blues, greens and soft purples of the glass that are his hallmark.

The glass is subjected to an iridescing process, which was rediscovered by one of Norman's colleagues during a visit to America where the Tiffany workshops once flourished. The pots are sprayed with a mixture of liquid chemicals, although *which* chemicals is a closely guarded secret. Personally I think Norman need have no fear, for although the effect is undoubtedly unusual and very lovely, it is Norman's own particular talent that makes them so unique. His use of colours, the way in which they blend and swirl one into another, some of them in uniform zig-zags and some in more abstract patterns, shows a talent particularly suited to the medium. Norman has a profound respect and real understanding of glass, born of years of working with it, for which there is no replacement.

When I went to visit him at his studio, he went through the whole process with me, talking all the while about every aspect of glass and blowing. It quickly became apparent, listening to him, that he is a man who has no interest in 'ART', he is a totally practical person whose passion lies in continually learning from, and discovering things about, glass and its properties. He told me "Glass is so fascinating because you seem to be working with a solid which is in fact a liquid." A pool of liquid glass is kept in a red hot furnace night and day and then a smaller furnace is used actually to produce the pot, plate, vase or whatever. The glass is held on an 'iron' and constantly turned; then taken out for short periods to shape it by hand with a wad of wet newspaper. It is a very hot business generally and the red hot furnaces looked quite frightening at first. As I watched a gorgeous iridescent blue bottle emerging, I felt it was rather like watching a magician at work at his alchemy. At first you have a rather sausagey lump of molten glass, then roll it in a few colours here and a few colours there, shape it a bit and hey presto, a bottle, almost more like a jewel than anything else, emerges.

Although Norman is obviously totally at home with his job, he has not always been a glassblower. At one time, before he met his wife, he worked on building sites and was a part-time lorry driver. But he says he always knew that he wanted to do something in art and eventually decided to go to night school to get the qualifications necessary to get into art school. This he managed to do, entering Middlesex Poly as a mature student, and it was no doubt here that his love and fascination with glass started. Having received his BA, he went on to work at a glassworks in his home county of Essex. Not long after, he started up the London Glassblowing Workshop with a colleague, Peter Layton, and it was during this period that Peter Layton came back from a trip to America with the incredible news that he had discovered the Tiffany 'secret'.

It was also during this time that one of those strange things that happen once in a lifetime, happened to Norman and his wife Dianne. They were down here on holiday and went to look at some pottery in Praze that a friend had recommended. It turned out that they were not only selling pots but also the house, studio and fields. Norman and Dianne fell in love with it and bought it almost there and then. Once they had moved Norman had to go about building his furnaces, something he had never done before. The furnaces are fed from two vast calor gas tanks outside the studio, which caused him sleepless nights at first; however nowadays they seem to have taken on a friendlier aspect and even their money-gobbling doesn't worry him as it did at first.

In fact, he is so busy these days, trying to keep up with orders from galleries, shops and forthcoming exhibitions, that he is considering taking on an assistant, "but it will have to be exactly the right person, although I know if I concentrate on it long enough someone will turn up," he says confidently.

He spends some of his precious time teaching people interested in glass blowing and enjoys this side of his work very much. "In a craft like this you can easily get into a rut. But with students, there is an interchange of ideas. It is the moving forward into new dimensions that I enjoy.".

At the moment, he is thinking along more sculptural lines and has made a few very organic-looking pieces that seem almost to grow out of the plates that they sit on. "I'm very interested in the shapes that glass naturally takes when it's in a molten state," he said, and it is obvious that this new direction is a whole new area of fascination for him.

If you are in the least interested in glass, or, dare I say it, art, I suggest that you go along to Praze-an-Beeble and take a look at Norman Stuart Clarke's work. I imagine that he is going to become a very collectable person in the future and if I wasn't a poverty-stricken journalist I would collect his work myself.

Jack Clemo

Kate Vaughan (August 1988)

Attempting to categorise Jack Clemo's poetry is an invidious exercise; his voice is as individual as the china-clay landscape he springs from. From there, and more recently from Dorset, he has spoken since the early 1950s, and this collection allows consideration of his output in a single volume of his own selections.

Two powerful concerns of his early work were religion and nature and the early poems are evidence of his continuous battling response with both. His faith was ultimately expressed out of his desolate heartland, the clay country, in the ravaged nature of which he found his personal good, encountering a truer vision of the suffering Christ in the clay-pit where "splintered wood and nails" spoke more eloquently than leaves and flowers.

His response to experience was puritanical, evangelical and impatient of formal religious ritual; his directness felt Christ's footsteps, the stain of His blood, the water springing from His side, to be marked in the clay landscape. Water dripping from machinery became the poet's baptism, and a cross formed by metal machinery a more direct frame for suffering. Clemo's distrust of Christian art, whose "symbols tempt simple souls like me," led to his prayer in *The Excavator* to "keep far from me all loveliness, O God, and let me laud Thy meaner moods."

Writing in the 1960s, many of his preoccupations remained the same. He had by now cruelly lost his sight which, together with his deafness, perpetuated his role as 'The Outsider', a man "full of strange fire," contemptuous of socialism and impatient with the veneer of order in the modern world. His powerful language and rich imagery were seemingly unaffected by his blindness. Around the time of his marriage to Ruth Peaty in 1968, his poems began to reach out to touch the lives of others, and he adopted the personae of mystics such as William Blake and T.F. Powys; Cornishmen Alfred Wallis and Billy Bray; Thomas Hardy and John Donne.

The poems of *Broad Autumn* continued this expansion and employed a greater range of themes, a mellowing of language and diversity of metre, and a gentler theology. *A Couple at Fowey* speaks both of the need to express beauty and laughter and also that Clemo is a "poet without nostalgia," whose mature writing was developing with lyrical acceptance the ability of natural beauty to reflect love. Much credit for this fulfilment must go to his wife, Ruth. The poem *Wedding Eve* is dedicated to her and speaks of a personal love grounded in personal faith.

His later poem *Whispers* explores a broader view of the Twentieth Century from a more tolerant standpoint than was possible in his early career; and in *Poem at Sixty* he reviews his past life and landscape, tracing his passage from

> "... the unschooled artist's
> crucible,
> The revivalist's platform,
> the hermit's cell,
> The theologian's tome open
> on granite,
> open to upland winds,
> And the sex mystic's pulse
> of moon-tokens
> on the loyal
> Pressed lips and breasts."

Jack Clemo has a clarity of vision and expression that those of us with all our senses intact might envy.

Photo: Jack with his wife, Ruth

Ian Cooke

Mike Venning (April 1986)

Ian Cooke comes from London. He did N.D.D. graphics at Kingston School of Art, which gave him a good grounding in many techniques but no job (catch 22—all graphics jobs required commercial experience; no experience, no job, conversely, no job, no experience!). So he got on with working at anything that came up. Eventually he set up his own letterpress and offset-litho business (one man band), printing raffle tickets, brochures, hand-bills etc.

He decided to sell up and move out into the country so chose St. Just because he could afford the price of house there. If John O'Groats had been cheaper he could easily have landed up there instead. That's an interesting point, for Ian's direction in life looks like a premeditated progression from urban bustle to specific rural retreat; whereas chance has played an important part in how things have gone. On getting to Penwith, Ian and his wife, Yuki, did all kinds of jobs, including cabbage cutting and potato picking. As a sideline, he made some lino prints which friends liked, and from there he started print-making.

He mixed what he remembered from art school with new learning of techniques, and progressed from there. The subject-matter of his first prints was rather picturesque and the landscape generalised, but the particular began to take over, and the Penwith moors and their covering of prehistoric stones became a major preoccupation. Chance had brought Ian into this area and started him print-making, yet an obvious empathy was present. This love of landscape has led him deeper and deeper into exploration of his surroundings and his own thoughts and feelings about them.

The prints themselves are studio creations, but the process begins with direct observation. He walks the moors constantly and makes drawings *in situ.* The drawings are the basic visual material for his prints. These are working drawings to be used for their information content. They provide the external references which connect with Ian's inner ideas and feelings in the creation of a print.

Ian uses two main print processes: lino-cut and etching; two contrasting techniques, but he handles both with consummate ease. He has a hand press which stands in the middle of his studio, along with the variety of rollers and other tools that he uses, all on display along with his prints. This is significant, indicating Ian's pride in all the aspects of his craft, and the importance he places on doing the whole thing himself. Men-an-Tol Studio itself also demonstrates this thoroughness. Ian fell in love with it, pursued and got it for a good price at auction and then Yuki and he created what they wanted it to be by themselves. He has even researched and written a pamphlet on the history of the building. The studio is open most days throughout the warm months of the year.

Until recently his work has continued to be realistic. In the last year, however, he has made radical changes and has produced prints which seem to reflect his own inner landscape as it relates to external stimuli such as Boscawen-un stone circle. His new prints are not naturalistic but more symbolic The designs are full of bright colour with areas of silver or gold foil which, when overprinted, appear embossed. Some of the symbolism in these prints may be universal but the meaning is what Ian personally sees, thinks and feels.

He has produced a useful and informative guidebook of the prehistoric remains that are in easy walking distance of his home. This fits into the process by which Ian communicates his love of the moors, the ancient stones and the mystery they still hold. Prints, writing, conversation: they all count. However, his theories and ideas are based as much on his own feelings as on his obvious research into the opinions of others.

Ian Cooke is very much his own man. His prints are evidence of his innermost thoughts, which he accepts as subjective, but as valid as anyone else's. He is not dogmatic. He is self-sufficient and has worked on his own terms to reach his present situation where he manages that rare feat of making a living out of his print-making.

Bob Devereux

Annette Robinson (September 1983)

Bob Devereux is not just a painter. He is not just a poet. Neither is he just a librettist, or a performer, or a gallery director. Specifically he is not any of these, but put them all together and he may appear. There again he may not. A new direction may have been taken, and this must be added to achieve a full picture. Rather like doing a jigsaw and never knowing until the last minute if you have all the pieces.

Two pieces look very much the same, but do not fit together. They are about abstract paintings, but only one is reaching out to speak. The first was conceived 18 years ago, an image born of a very different time. Bob Devereux was then a graphic artist running his own advertising agency. He had studied at the Kingston College of Art, and afterwards had visions of opening a gallery which would provide a much-needed outlet for the students at the college. This did not reach fruition, and instead, 2 years later, Bob turned his hand to graphics in the commercial world of advertising. He manipulated words and images to sell products, but this was a far cry from the heart of the artist. At night the pure abstract forms were created. "Symbols of escape, of flight, of breaking down walls," that were not intended to communicate on any literary or figurative level. They were a private statement. Only now, after all these years, have these forms reappeared, but now they draw us in to share an experience, these images of movement, of flight. The walls have been broken down.

If these two pieces are put on either side of the picture, we can try to link the centre pieces to them. 1967-71 was to be a period of non-painting. Bob gave up advertising and moved down to Cornwall, only to find that his painting in no way related to his new situation. In this new environment he could not find any reference to the shapes he had been using, but he could not bring himself to paint figuratively. Realism at that point seemed like selling out his ideals but he believed that people would buy his work because it represented what they saw, like a postcard or a photograph—simply a souvenir. It was a time of struggle.

In 1969 Bob bought a Heidelberg Printing Press, with the intention of printing poetry books and ultimately fine art prints, but things went wrong. Orders had started to come in, but despite this the bank would no longer support the business, and Bob was left with a debt to pay off on the initial investment.

To help with his finances Bob became a deckchair attendant on St Ives Harbour front, working from 7.30am to 6.00pm, and then working as a waiter in the evenings. He still found time, however, to involve himself in the organisation of cultural activities, as he does today. In 1970 he helped to organise a fringe festival for St Ives which involved 230 performers from all over the region. It brought with it some personal success for Bob because of his poetry readings, which he performed with Jim Hughes, accompanying him on guitar. They were invited to tour university circuits and clubs during the winter months, performing under the name of 'Mask'. In 1971 they were joined by violinist Bridget Tickner, and they toured each winter until 1973. They won a silver cup at the Slough Music Festival, and as a direct result one of the judges, Frances Line, invited them to do a half-hour programme in the Sounds on Sunday series on Radio 2. The group had a manager who was anxious to sign proper contracts, but Bob refused to sign since it would have meant travelling full-time. The split was inevitable, and another chapter closed, but Bob has never given up performing. He was soon working with Clive Palmer (ex Incredible String Band), and from 1976-78 they performed regular cabaret spots at the Pudding Bag Restaurant in St Ives. In 1979 the group Rhombus was formed, with Dick Reynolds and Tim Wellard joining the duo.

Bob started painting again while he was working on the deckchairs, a job he continued each summer. He found he could not write at this time, and spending his days on the harbour front he became aware that "the painter is not recording a moment in time, as the camera does, but the experience of the whole period of time that he is sitting in front of the subject." He picked up his brush, and has been painting ever since. For two seasons he refused to sell anything because he felt the need to consolidate the new direction his work had taken. By 1972 he was ready to exhibit, and a small exhibition of harbour paintings (watercolours) was held in St Ives library, and it was a virtual sell-out.

Having made the decision to "live painting without compromise" he opened a stall in the Sloop Craft Market in 1973, opened the Salt House Gallery in 1980, and in August this year opened another room, adding further dimension and scope. His deckchair/beach-hut paintings immediately come to mind as an example of his work in recent years, eye-catching, with their freedom of colour and movement of brush, but again they are a part of the jigsaw that can never be complete. The abstract forms that fill his most recent paintings show that change is ever present, and moving forward all the time.

This brings us to the present, with only one piece left. Bob and his family have recently move to a large barn in St Erth, and are in the process of developing it into a home for themselves, and a cultural centre with a large studio. It looks out onto a landscape that is enclosed on the distant boundaries by tall trees and an abundance of flourishing wilderness, and within that enclosure a feeling of space, of movement, of flight, leading ever outwards to freedom—not a wall in sight.

During the last four years Bob Devereux has been collaborating with the classical composer, Christopher Brown. Their first commission 'Seascape' was a choral work performed at the St Ives Festival '81. Since then they have written a children's opera 'King Ram' which was performed at the Midlands Art Centre, Birmingham, in 1982. They are currently working on an opera, about a plague village in Derbyshire called Eyam, which has been commissioned by the Arts Council

Julian Dyson

Ashley Peters (December 1988)

Julian Dyson was born in St Mawes, Cornwall, in 1936. His father was a doctor and was keen for him to have a profession, so Julian became a dentist. He was in general practice dentistry up country for nearly 20 years, but kept painting and drawing in every available hour

Something had to give and so eight years ago, he gave up the general practice. He is now totally committed to painting and these days limits himself to a little dentistry, visiting geriatric and handicapped people. After years of wanting to return to St Mawes to live, he finally made it back home in 1985.

He is a self-taught painter and has always been preoccupied with the actual qualities of paint and surface. He admires these qualities in the work of Francis Bacon: likes the way he arranges his figures—almost stage-like—and the use of colour. However, the admiration stops there. He does not relate to Bacon's imagery.

Dyson's subject matter is inspired by his place of birth: it is of the people who inhabit the streets and pubs of St Mawes and of the landscape and seascape which he sees from every corner.

Wistfulness and nervousness combine in some of his paintings. They feel on the edge of life. In one, a young girl is in the process of growing up, looking, a little frightened, towards a window. In another, titled *Oscar,* a local man who has lost his arm in an accident, this wistfulness is the link between the man and the bird. There is also an acute sense of isolation in many of his works, but it is blended with tenderness. Dyson draws and paints from experience. There is a painting of a lonely old man sitting in a chair in the TV room of a seedy hotel. Dyson used to see him there from noon until midnight. Every day, day after day. This loneliness is reinforced by his use of sparse and plain backgrounds. He sees that underneath the surface of society there are an awful lot of lonely creatures, yet he himself is not a lonely person.

In St Mawes, he feels this strong division between the people. There are the rich and retired, for whom he has little time, and the working people of the village. Fully expressed in his paintings is a sympathy for the less well-off, while the rich are gently caricatured.

He knows St Mawes intimately. The business of Cornishness over there is tinged with the problems of lack of housing. The rich can spend terrific amounts on houses, leaving nothing for local people and this creates a tension between both sides.

Dyson recalls a story about a chap who is a figure in one of his public bar paintings. Over at St Mawes, this man was nicknamed 'Shoes'. Rich, retired, one of the sort who comes and goes. He got into the yachting and shooting side of life, bought all the right equipment and clothing, lived about two years down here and then went back to where he came from. For him, the winters were too cold, too long and too *wet.* He was a kind man but he was fond of talking about money. He talked about how expensive his shoes were and how they took a year to make. Some wag replied, "Well, it gave you time to save up, then."

Another incident: Dyson saw a young couple walking down the street on a lovely summer's day. The man was wearing a flat tweed cap, a barbour coat, a white scarf and green wellingtons. Five yards behind him was a woman wearing the same. To Dyson, they were a couple of ducks.

He finds a great wealth of characters in St Mawes, plenty of material for him to work on.

His sense of humour permeates a number of his paintings. *The Couple is* based on an old photograph printed in a magazine. Vanderbilt, the man who owned much of the US railways, was about 70 in the photo and still had a penchant for young girls. Dyson saw him as a man just buying another commodity. The young girl, on the other hand, was winning the jackpot, financially. The hand around her arm in the painting is like a rat's claw. The man s head is hard and bullish; she wears a sickly-sweet smile. The relationship between them is an empty one.

This theme, of a lack of human rapport, occurs again in other paintings. He watches the heavy drinkers in the pubs. He paints scenes in which one person will be talking on in a monologue, with another doing the same, neither relating to the other at all A lot of his figures seem to be balding and middle-aged or old. Their flesh is ruddy and rough.

Dyson's palette used to be limited to bold, bright, primary colours, but these days his colours are becoming less strident. Blues are among his favourites. Since the paint surface is very important to him, he finds the faster he paints the better the painting. His recent paintings were executed quickly and this gives them a feeling of movement and freshness.

Drawing is very important to him and this can be seen in his paintings which have strong, linear qualities. Nearing the end of a painting, he comes back to the black line around a figure, or an edge of a floor, or a window.

At first glance, his paintings feel quite spare, spacious, with not a lot going on in them. In fact, the more you stay with them, the more you see of a story woven around the characters.

He still finds painting difficult and a struggle. He finds that if it comes too easily, it somehow lacks something, lacks sweat.

He has made St Mawes his territory. Dyson's paintings are solid, strong and vital: he gets under the skin of the people, the landscape and the seascape he's portraying.

Julian Dyson's exhibition at The Salthouse, St Ives, has just finished, but one or two of his paintings can always be seen upstairs at this gallery.

Article taken from a conversation between Julian Dyson and Bob Devereaux by Ashley Peters.

John Emanuel

Mike Venning (May 1986)

Change is a gradual process for John Emanuel, two steps forward and one back, as he put it. His work moves forward with care; change and progress are inevitable but must be considered, each movement re-evaluated. No leaps in the dark. Yet his life has seen one such leap, from a straightforward existence in Barrow-in-Furness without any involvement in art, to painting in St. Ives. He sees this as influenced by the changing mood of the 'sixties, any decisiveness also tempered by the fact that a friend who was already in St. Ives suggested that he come down, so he did, and has been there ever since.

He painted at home while labouring to pay the bills. He didn't exhibit much and found himself being very critical of his own work, destroying all but the very best. He looks on a lot of that work as learning the ropes; trying things out and picking up useful advice from other artists. Advice which has proved most helpful when it has concerned practical tips. Theoretical talk for him always seems to stay in the realm of theory, and doesn't come down to earth to be of use in the business of putting paint to canvas.

Painting is the bottom line for John Emanuel. It is the end towards which all of his creativity is directed. He has always painted figures, sometimes in landscape, occasionally venturing into pure landscape though always with anthropomorphic overtones. The figures in his earlier work were stylised and the paintings monochromatic. Recently the figures have become realistic and he has introduced more and more colour.

For a long time he liked to preserve a sense of anonymity about. the figures in his paintings. He concentrated on the shapes of the body; faces, hands and feet were often absent and while human form was always evident, the paintings worked as strong abstract compositions. Now John is concerned with the whole figure. Identity is important. He wants to portray the whole person of his subject, his own thoughts and feelings, and the relationship between the artist and his model.

There are technical similarities to past work: thick paint with subtle overworking, strong shapes. But the increased use of colour has produced new considerations. Whereas paintings used to be pulled together by unity of shape and colour, he now works with bright, sharp areas of colour which contrast with and break up the nuances of tone and texture of the body. He sees the next development in this direction as the addition of identifiable background which will set up more contrasts and present him with more definable subject-matter to be pulled together in a unified. composition.

He works in two distinct stages. Firstly he draws from life, mostly in ink with colour wash. These drawings are spontaneous and gestural, done at speed and quite loose. They provide the bridge between the subject and the painting yet are not just working drawings. He exhibits them and they should be enjoyed along with the paintings as they show a lighter, more carefree side of John Emanuel's personality.

John works on his paintings with reference to his drawings. Being one step removed from the live model, they are more subjective, emerging from that strange process-cum-fight between the artist, his materials and his innermost self that seems to be the birth-process of most art. External references are subjugated by the dictatorship of the painting as a whole. He sometimes uses a third process to aid his vision by making small clay figurines from which he draws in order to get another perspective on the human figure.

John's work has many contrasting, almost paradoxical elements. The considered, structured paintings can be set against the quick, calligraphic marks and freely-applied, often brilliant, colours of the drawings. Also he sees his work as moving in depth through a restricted area of subject-matter, yet within these supposedly narrow confines he manages to deal with a wide spread of artistic problems. More evidence of apparent paradox can be seen in his studio where a large, yellowing newspaper cutting about Barnett Newman, a cerebral and thoroughly non-figurative painter, is pinned up. Most incongruous, one thinks, then the connection is made: the painting as an object independent of external references overrides all other considerations. John Emanuel, in his quiet, careful way, covers a lot of ground and, for him, the painting is paramount.

His most recent work is exhibited at the Salthouse Gallery in St. Ives until May 7th, the selection containing good examples of both his painting and drawing.

Laurie Finestone

Annette Robinson (May 1983)

Laurie Finestone specialises in etching. She has lived in Penzance for two years, and is a member of the Newlyn Society of Artists. She will be having her own exhibition in the Newlyn Orion Gallery from 31st May to 2nd July, and is also exhibiting some of her work in the Bath Festival from 28th May. Her past exhibitions include showings at the Festival Gallery, Bath; West of England Academy, Bristol; Spacex Gallery, Exeter; Plymouth Arts Centre; Mall Gallery, London; Penzance Arts Centre; Bristol Museum and the 35 King Street Gallery, Bristol .

Laurie first started working with the techniques of etching in Italy. She moved to Florence in 1971, and spent two and a half years in an environment that inspired and motivated her artistic mind. There she found a way of life that lent itself perfectly to creativity. There was a richness of life, the people cared about craftsmanship, and the awareness of art was an integral part of people's lives. The materials she could buy there were superior in quality, and a sense of pride and respect was always present. This, then, was the environment in which Laurie started her etchings, working in the Santa Reparata Graphics Studio in Florence. Towards the end of her stay she exhibited at the Palazzo Strozzi Gallery, her individual style already apparent, and what better place to launch herself into the round of galleries than one in a city so much in tune with the world of art.

Next Laurie moved to Bath. She spent a few months looking for a studio to work in, and used this time to learn other crafts, such as pottery, silkscreen, and raku. During her seven years in Bath, she also used these skills, along with photography, to experiment with the inter-relationship of different techniques. In her experience this opens the mind to different ideas, and these ideas can be carried out in creative ways. She would like to put together an exhibition to show how this can be achieved, at a later date .

Eventually Laurie found the beginnings of a co-operative workshop in Bristol. It was a venture in its very early stages called the Bristol Print-making Co-operative, and Laurie helped to establish it and continued to work there for the best part of seven years. It involved about thirty people, and it is still going strong today. Not like the early days: it took at least four years before galleries started to approach them, and it must have been hard and thankless work at times. They managed to get a grant from South West Arts for a press, and were also helped by them to put together a portfolio to help to promote their work.

Now that Laurie lives in Penzance she has a studio in her own home. She continues to produce a very high standard of work. For example, her series of black and white etchings include a feast of intricate line work, and they deserve close observation to pick out the interesting and often very amusing details that decorate the larger framework which at first catches the eye. This is also apparent in her smaller etchings and drawings, some of which are not in her exhibitions. They deserve a mention, however, because they show how meticulously each one is carried out, down to the smallest print on a tablecloth. Each one maintains a light-heartedness that can be felt throughout all of her work.

Although a lot of Laurie Finestone's work is in black and white, she has used limited colour to tone and enhance some of her etchings. These immediately take on another dimension, and are visually striking because of it. The colours are not vivid, instead they create a background for patterns, and accentuate shape and form. They in no way dominate the finished work, they simply add warmth and depth.

Her son Miles, who is eight, has been a constant source of inspiration, from being the subject engaged in various pastimes, to having his own drawings shown as pictures on the walls. In her painting "Making pinch pots in the garden" the softness of line and simple detail (in contrast to her etchings) lend themselves fully to bring out the natural way that a child adapts itself to its creative activity. It shows complete concentration and the ability of a child to be totally engrossed and at one with its work or play. The picture has a gentle, timeless feel about it, and could easily bring childhood memories flooding back.

Make sure that you go and see her work at the Newlyn Orion in June. You will come away feeling positively refreshed!

Michael Finn

Lu Simmons (September 1989)

At last, Michael Finn is beginning to get the recognition he deserves, with a large exhibition at the Newlyn Gallery running from September 16th to October 21st, a powerful show last year at the Salthouse Gallery, and another booked at Wolf at the Door in 1990.

Although Michael was only 16 when he was first overwhelmed by a painting in the Tate and fell in love with the magic of that particular kind of make-believe, and although the desire to make that kind of magic has stayed with him all his life, it was not until 1982 that he was in a position to become a full-time painter.

The intervening years saw Michael as a pilot, studying art at the Royal College, teaching at Somerset College of Art, and being Principal of both Falmouth School of Art and Bath Academy of Art, a pretty daunting career and one in which painting had to take a back seat, to be undertaken only during college holidays.

It was a toss-up for Michael whether to follow his love of painting or his second love, flying, and although painting won him back after the war, the feelings of space, peace and eternity that were with him in the clouds are very much present in his paintings today.

Just after the war, Michael remembers seeing the American Exhibition, and was very influenced by the scale of what he saw and by the minimal work seen in the show. However, it was not until 1971 that he discovered for himself that the less he put in a painting, the more it said back to himself and others. Since then, he has been trying to paint pictures with very little apparent content, but which express the strength of his feelings; paintings that say something about being quiet, that you can look at every day not to find something new in the detail, but to come to look on and love as an old friend.

Some of these paintings have almost no colour change and minimal marks and it would be very easy for people to dismiss them as they hurry past But they would be missing so much the power and integrity, the warmth and the magic. Instead of hurrying past, give these paintings time, allow them to draw you into the layers of paint, many of which you only get to glimpse tantalisingly, or the marks of now-covered brush strokes which occasionally can be seen in certain lights. All these hint at the fact that often these paintings came about very, very slowly. As Michael says, they have to be painted as unselfconsciously as possible in order for them to work. "I gradually realise what I am doing, having done it!"

Michael admits that it is "difficult to know why one is drawn in a particular direction, why one is drawn to do things which are difficult to express in words." But, while he is working, he can almost feel the painting telling him how to paint it. If he kicks against this intuitive sense, nothing happens and the painting goes out onto the bonfire!

This strong sense of intuition can be seen in the following story: Alongside the paintings Michael makes crucifixes. It was a request from his son Richard, for a small pectoral cross made by his father, that first started Michael in this direction. Richard did not get his small cross, but rather a huge, heavy crucifix in mauves, blues white and black.

Later, when Richard was going to Cambridge, he asked his father for a more portable crucifix to take with him, and Michael made him one. He was, at that time, taking up wooden door risers in order to put down fitted carpets and it was this wood that gave him the idea for the new crucifix. It turned out to resemble a figure standing in front of a crucifix, preaching, and the figure was painted black.

Three years later, Richard joined the Dominican Order, whose habit is white, covered with long, black surplices. What an intuitive father!

Michael has three children—two daughters and a son—and confesses lovingly that he is so glad to have them. From his late teens, he had an overwhelming desire to be married and to have children, "I didn't realise that it happened to men, that you actually felt the *need* to have children." Although all three have left home now, there is still a tremendously close family bond, with Michael and Cely providing the loving, stable background and the caring home that is still frequently visited.

Michael is a quietly religious man, born and bred a Catholic, and says that "it does something to you for life, enabling you to put things in a particular kind of perspective, in that you learn early that you have a role to play in life." The role is not always easy; life is to enjoy, but occasionally one has to suffer—the bread does not always fall butter up!

After many years of having to teach to earn a living, of having to cope with the problems of students experimenting with drugs, of being in a position of authority when the 'sixties was a time for kicking over the traces and revolution was always bubbling away at the surface, Michael Finn has finally found himself fulfilling his life-long ambition: "The right thing to do is to be a full-time painter, if you can."

Michael Finn is one of today's strongest painters. So, slow down, see the show and draw from it some of his particular magic.

Robert Floyd

Mike Venning (June 1986)

Robert Floyd knew the direction he wanted to take with painting while at Art College and followed it. This had its problems and partly prompted him to change college in mid-course. Since that move, which proved a good one, he has continued painting in the way he wants with a quiet calm which seems to hide great strength and determination.

After college, a friend's decision to come to St. Ives brought him there. He didn't actually know what to expect until he arrived, in fact he felt like returning home to Birmingham when he got to Hayle! However, he's stayed in St. Ives and finds it a very congenial place. An attractive aspect for him is the safety of the streets and freedom from the paranoia that seems a permanent part of present-day city life.

Robert's always been painting but his wife, Carol, had done enamel work at college so they both set to enamelling as a way to use their talents to earn a living. This they have done and have a workshop and sales space in the Sloop craft market. His enamels, particularly the landscapes, are delicate and demonstrate the same care and attention to detail that is found in his paintings. While painting is his main concern, enamelling is not dismissed as some kind of hack work.

The paintings are multi-layered yet appear deceptively straightforward. One's first impression is of realism achieved with incredible patience and care. However this is only one level and may be a superficial one at that. Some paintings appear at first glance to seem non-representational. This happens through Robert's use of close-up figures only partly in the picture, coupled with inanimate subject-matter such as venetian blinds, surfboards and railings which can easily appear as abstract patterns and shapes. A painting of a surfer's leg clad in multi-coloured wet-suit, a part of his decorated surfboard and the sea spray can look almost abstract expressionist at a glance, although when the subject is recognised it is supremely realistic.

It's not a case of visual tricks in the paintings. Many are quite unambiguous visually, yet their apparent blandness creates a tension in that the spectator's imagination is put to work. Figurative art always presents a puzzle to the onlooker. Who is this person? Why are they as they are in the painting? Robert says that he finds a face looking out of the picture creates difficulties of composition because it draws all the attention and becomes too strong a focus. Thus his paintings mostly contain a single figure looking away, partially obscured, or in back view. An air of mystery is produced which has affinities with surrealism, particularly the deadpan but disturbing paintings of Magritte, not that one would make any direct comparisons, nor call Robert Floyd a surrealist. Nevertheless, since the advent of surrealism, representational painting inevitably contains an additional edge of psychological tension .

The physical fact of paint on canvas in Robert's work is important. The figures may be realistic but they are obviously and purposely the result of painstaking brushwork. The paint may be applied with care and precision, but the pictures are neither *trompe l'oeil* nor hyper-realism. They do not pretend to be anything but paintings. In fact he feels himself changing to a more painterly style making more gestural use of paint. He sees this as a gradual process, no likelihood of instant action painting, but a departure towards new ways of expression is underway.

The process of change taking place now can be tied in with a constant movement away from the technical expertise and graphic quality of his earlier work towards a more subtle expression of the levels of meaning present in his paintings. Like his work, Robert is cool and calm, yet neither is cold and unemotional. The pictures have a relaxed feel, but are not the product of a detached observer, nor a bland exterior hiding seething mania. They don't stand still either, and it will be most interesting to see the end-results of the changes happening in Robert Floyd's work now.

Anthony Frost

Mike Venning (February 1986)

Anthony Frost was born in St. Ives, but lived in various places as a child. Late teenage found him in Oxfordshire where he did his Art School foundation course at Banbury, finishing his, institutional art education at Cardiff Art College.

He then returned to West Cornwall and has remained, painting full-time, ever since. He sees this as quite natural, almost inevitable, while accepting that his wife Linda's job with its regular income has certainly made his choice more easy. At the same time Anthony looks after Luke and Danny, their sons. He is also a visiting lecturer at Canterbury Art School and has taught at Falmouth Art School. As a painter he has exhibited around the country for many years in group shows and solo.

The Frosts live near Morvah in a cottage filled with paintings and bright colours. Wind and sea are permanently in the background, while inland the ground rises craggily towards Watch Croft and the Galvers. Anthony's studio in Newlyn also commands a terrific view over Newlyn harbour and east across Mount's Bay. It is ironic to mention all this, which you can't miss when visiting Anthony, because his painting has nothing to do with landscape or any sort of external object or subject.

Anthony Frost loves paint and colour. He is an abstract painter and his work has no external references at all. Colour is important in all of his paintings; he uses it with great skill and verve, and takes risks with it. You are never faced with something safe and tasteful but a living mass of colours, some clashing, while others harmonise. Yet each painting is complete in itself, and each shape or mass of colour fits the whole, sometimes only just! This is exactly where the excitement lies for both Anthony and the viewer who is left at times wondering how he got away with it.

He always starts from a basic structure. He did write phrases and words on the canvas and work from that, also domino and playing-card patterns, the latter supplying a recurrent theme of diamonds. Now he begins with a simple structure of canvas or cardboard pieces stuck onto board or canvas which serve as a framework for the paint This can all but disappear in the mass of rich colour which is the painting. The paint might however accentuate one part of the structure, while obliterating another.

The structure is positioned in a kind of controlled accident, the pieces of canvas or card being dropped onto the painting surface and mostly stuck down as they lie, but he does admit to a slight degree of control over the composition. The paint then takes over, he works with acrylic, often very thick, and lays it on with brush or palette knife. The act of painting is a total commitment, he obviously makes decisions about colour and shape but works quickly, pulling the painting together by constantly changing it; adding, deleting, until it works as a whole.

Titles are important, maybe the title comes first, or maybe the painting. The title feels right for the painting but there's no direct reference. A title may hang around in his head or be written down in a notebook before the right painting occurs Likewise a painting may have to wait, unnamed, for the right title, or have its title changed until something really fits.

Anthony listens to music or to the radio when he is painting, and picks up many of his titles from lines of songs or perhaps a radio play. Music is something that affects his frame of mind when painting, but he's not trying to produce a visual equivalent of what he hears. His favourite music is the Fall and Captain Beefheart who produce sounds and statements which seem particularly right to him. Both can be raw and honest, and they take risks with music just as Anthony does with paintings. But Anthony's paintings are not illustrations, nor even impressions of mood influenced by music.

The new paintings are looser and more gestural than his previous work. They are fresh, often dazzling and full of movement; definitely not visual muzak. In my opinion this is his best work yet. It will appear in his one-man show at Newlyn Orion Gallery from February 19 to March 15. He will also do children's workshops at the gallery, which seems an excellent idea to accompany any exhibition, especially when the artist is as lively and stimulating as Anthony Frost!

Terry Frost

Mike Venning (March 1986)

On entering Terry Frost's present exhibition at the Newlyn Orion, I was hit with the sheer intensity of yellow pouring from the large painting 'Black Sun'. After a moment of recovery from this blast, I found colours, contrasts and movement reverberating all around the walls from a collection of paintings radiating exuberance. Certainly not a case of a genteel decline along with the ageing process. It doesn't seem to be that way with painters, they just take more risks, and often become more brash than ever.

Painting in the '80s? Terry is in his early seventies now and the pictures, like the man, are overflowing with life and energy. Perhaps that story of the dip in Aphrodite's Pool and its rejuvenating effects should be taken seriously!

His conversation sparkles too; hilarious anecdotes abound, punctuated by loud laughter, yet his comments on art are pithy and straight to the point.

Terry Frost's attitude to art, and life, is one of wholehearted involvement. He seems to have thrown himself with gusto into everything that he's done. His paintings are an obvious example of this. His other main activities may not provide such apparent evidence, but the enthusiasm is always there. He is a natural teacher, the information just flows out of him, and, before you know it, you're considering his words with the intention of experimenting when the next opportunity of grabbing a brush or pencil arrives. Teaching has been a practical consideration, it was a means of providing for a large family. But, as often happens, one conscious reason hides a deeper need, and teaching hasn't just been a way to keep the kids in shoes and the larder stocked.

"When I am painting, I am not concerned with theory however much thinking I may have done before I started to paint. When I am really painting—no! I cannot describe that, for all I know is that as soon as I realise I have been painting I have stopped. I am only concerned with what I am to do next. When I do paint I am discovering what I have to do. Thought for me is before and after but not at the time. When one is thinking there are so many possibilities. When one paints one *knows;* and the statement is definite. Granted some statements are better than others. That's it! That's why I paint."

Painting for Terry is all to do with seeing and experiencing. He doesn't consider his work as 'abstract'. Everything he paints is the result of observation and its accompanying thoughts and emotions. He may be looking at Newlyn harbour, or catching a chance glimpse of waning moon and rising sun together in the dawn sky over Cyprus. The art, however, is nothing to do with getting a likeness or copying. Images are allowed to settle in his mind and what appears on canvas is the result of a mix within him. And then again it's not that easy, just as the painting is not a copy of what is seen, nor is it a copy of something in his mind.

Colour and contrast are important to Terry. Here again he is neither theoretic nor totally non-representational. The yellow rectangles towards the top of 'Black Sun' were suggested by the bright yellow shapes of Suttons' fish lorries parked on the quayside at Newlyn. The black circles occurring in various paintings were olives heated and fed to him by a Cypriot bar-owner as an antidote for a surfeit of Ouzo. So he is not a purist colour painter, while enjoying more and more the sheer pleasure and challenge of using undiluted hues with a limited vocabulary of forms.

He has been working throughout the post-war period and his knowledge of the art and artists of this time is wide. While the stories may be funny, the insight is deep, and anyway, the hard, serious work of painting needs humour for balance. He has a humanitarian breadth of experience, the humour is never cruel, and he knows a good painting or painter when he sees one.

Enough of this. Terry Frost's recent paintings are in the Orion Gallery now and more words won't provide a single clue to them. There's always more to say, but over to Terry for an apt riposte to that. . .

"I am convinced that people who just look for words to describe art completely miss what is in a good work, for words describe the known image; good art is indescribable and that is why it's usually an irritant: Because it is really indescribable, it retains a freedom for the artist."

Robin Giddey

Pam Otto (March 1988)

Robin Giddey is a rare man. Born in New Southgate in London, the grandson of a chef who worked under Escoffier, he was reared in the traditions of service 'old style' and they have never left him. He is at home in this but, unlike countless others in his walk of life, he has a temperament that in the bad old days would have marked him as a highly prized butler. Of pride and self-esteem he has plenty, but to take orders from others is his natural role. Under his waiter's jacket and brylcreemed hair there lurks a man who has understood equality in a manner which many of us never master.

His grandfather, having trained at the Carlton, went on to own restaurants in Geneva and elsewhere in Switzerland. And it was in Geneva that Robin, at the age of fifteen, came to train. Here he learnt all aspects of waiting and the restaurant business under the strict and watchful eyes of his two grandparents.

When the war broke out he returned to England and took up occupancy at Caxton Hall in Yorkshire, again as a waiter but this time serving illustrious American generals and brigadiers. During this time he was called upon to serve General Lord Mountbatten his breakfast in bed and to wait upon Princess Alexandra. The intimacy of such situations would leave an indelible impression on any man and Robin recalls them with great pleasure and pride.

After the war Robin went to find his fortune in London and find it he did, being employed by the Ritz, for very little money but enormous prestige. Here he trained under a man named Frank Maggin, who he worked with for almost thirty years until he left London. After his probationary term in the restaurant he was put in the Rivoli Bar and there he stayed for the next seventeen years, learning everything about cocktails that there is to know. The Ritz was famed for the driest Dry Martinis in town, and to see Robin perform this task makes your alcoholic taste buds tingle.

Those were the days when Lords and Ladies had their private silver brought in for private parties not wanting to sully their hands with the inferior stuff that the Ritz had to offer. "It wasn't that inferior though, I can tell you" says Robin with a twinkle in his eye. His customers were the richest and mightiest in the world: Ali Khan, the son of the Aga Khan, Paul Getty, Sir John Mills, Omar Sharif, the list runs on and on. Harold Macmillan would pop in for a quick drink after having his hair cut by the Ritz barbers. Paul Getty drank small rum and cokes and always had a different girl with him; Omar Sharif drank neat Russian vodka.

Eventually, in 1969, Frank Maggin and all his staff decided that prestige was all very well but good wages were better and decamped to the slightly less up-market regions of Bond Street and the Westbury Hotel. Here they took over the horsy domain of the Polo Bar, much frequented by actors, film-stars and the occasional politician.

It is in the nature of a barman's job that he will get to know his regular clients well. Within the hallowed precincts of that alcoholic haze, many a secret will be shared and Robin became the confidante of the rich and famous. Omar Sharif would come alone and sit for hours discussing his favourite topics of racing and bridge. Tom Jones would come in with his son and enjoy a bottle of Dom Perignon after seeing his agent across the road in Conduit Street. George Brown was another who would come in, always alone, and sit chatting, whose company Robin particularly enjoyed. However, Robin Is that most prized of confidantes, a silent one, and whatever passed between these men and himself will forever remain a mystery because Robin to this day is keeping mum. And to slur another man's character doesn't come under the rules of Robin's code.

In 1978, he and his wife Roberta decided that much as they enjoyed their by now wealthy life style, the glamour and razzmatazz of London was wearing thin and that it was time for a change. So they set off in their car to find themselves a small hotel to buy, finally arriving in Penzance and one of the larger bed and breakfasts in Alexandra Road. They liked Penzance immediately and having since tried other areas in Cornwall now know that here they will stay.

Robin says that they have no nostalgia for the faster world of London and no desire to return and although they do take occasional holidays to visit his relatives in Geneva; the lifestyle of West Penwith suits them very well.

Of course they are not nearly as well off as they once were, this worries them not at all, being compensated for by the more relaxed atmosphere of their working lives and the charm of the surrounding countryside.

When Robin was new at the Union he was considered by many of the clientele to be very stiff and starchy and no fun at all, but since then many of them have begun to enjoy the sense of irony in his 'hammy' bartender's performance and to understand that under it lies a heart. One perhaps ought to take into consideration what we must have looked like to him; this, after all, is the man who, faced with a classy French couple ordering cocktails before their meal in the Union Restaurant, chatted politely with them in fluent French .

So next time you are drunkenly ordering your fifth round of Bass; remember just who it is that you are speaking to. If you're very lucky he might just mix you one of his famous cocktails, like the superlative Union Cocktail he mixed for me.

John Halkes

Martin Val Baker (April1991)

After sixteen years in probably the most influential position in the Cornwall arts world, Newlyn Orion director John Halkes has resigned to take up a position as an independent arts consultant. We visited him at his home in Sancreed to reflect on the Halkes years at Newlyn.

I asked John if he had ever put on things he didn't like. "I think I've been disappointed a number of times. Something may look good in advance, but when it arrives you realise that it isn't. But you have to stand by it – you can't win them all."

Suggestions for exhibitions would often come from members, but John made the final decisions on the programmes, which were taken first to the management and then to the Arts Council or SWA. Balance was very important, with a wariness of too many thematic or large solo shows. Mixed shows often caused the most problems.

John has felt that women artists have been badly treated over the years, and noted the emergence of some very fine artists in the last decade. He is particularly proud of the major solo shows by Gillian Ayres and Jennifer Durrant. However, he doesn't believe in 'women's art' or 'male art' and rather than put on a mixed women's exhibition, he would look for some theme other than gender. In fact, some of the strongest regional artists showing at Newlyn now are women and that was not so ten or fifteen years ago.

He feels the area is very lucky to have independent galleries such as Wolf at the Door and The Salthouse to complement Newlyn Orion and the Penwith Gallery. "For example, the major Michael Finn exhibition at Newlyn could only have been shown or resourced properly by a subsidised gallery, but I hoped that it would support the smaller show at the Wolf at the Door, which was equally super but in a different context. Very often we were pointed towards good artists by the smaller galleries and, having run one, I have nothing but the utmost respect for them. I think they do an enormous amount for the district – I just wish that there was a more buoyant economy."

Did he have to try and balance commerce and reputation as they did? "The programme of a subsidised gallery should not be shaped by its commercial potential – the whole idea is to free one from that pressure – but over the years self-generated income has become an important part of the funding package. It seemed to me that we had to go for it. There were occasions when, looking at the balance of the three-year plan, I was able to pull in something which had local appeal. It was fine tuning, really. It used to be thought of as a dirty business, the subsidised sector selling art, but I was all for a sense of reality from the start – we were accepting credit cards by the later 'Seventies! I have always maintained that being subsidised does not release you from your responsibility to support the arts."

As the major gallery in the area, the pressure from artists for space to exhibit and sell must be tremendous. They are rather touchy people. He must have needed great tact to deal with a surfeit of exhibitors?

"Yes, that was one of the most difficult parts of the job because you are dealing with people's life work and you have to say no far more frequently than you say yes. There was also a large number who came to the gallery for help and advice, a role that we took on formally as a way of getting to know the newcomers. But yes, one is besieged ... a major pressure is from people who have a mid-career block and who see a solo show at Newlyn as the way out because of the colour brochure and the radio and TV coverage."

He is rarely seen at Private Views. Did he ever go to exhibitions for pleasure rather than business?

"I've just been to the Stanley Spencer exhibition at the Barbican – it was super. One of the problems is that you get a bit jaded. If you are seriously looking at art, private views are not really the right time. Sometimes I go to support an artist, but that can be seen as partisan. I worked very hard at the job and preferred to see the shows quietly, or often in the artist's studio – that's where I really loved to see the work."

Does he think that his sixteen years at Newlyn was long enough?

"Yes – slightly longer than it should have been, perhaps. But we were at a crucial stage of the development of our relationship with the County Council and at that time I thought it sensible to stay on. Recently there was pressure from SWA to develop a new policy – they were stating that they wanted to see a more contemporary avant garde programme and there was a feeling that Newlyn was a bit 'safe' – whatever that means. The public doesn't see it like that, but that's the way the arts bureaucrats speak. I felt that after the past three years – having established certain goals but sadly having lost the argument over the development plan – the gallery needed a fresh input of expertise. Really, Newlyn now needs – and I am pleased to say seems to have acquired – someone younger. I started this in my mid-thirties and now I'm fifty-one!"

Does he feel that Newlyn Orion was his baby? Would he be cross if the new director changed things?

"It's difficult. I've got over the 'bereavement' that goes with this sort of thing. You have to accept that whatever happens now is not your responsibility. You cannot go on hugging it to your chest and making it difficult for the people who have to carry it forward. I have to say, though, that I would be extremely upset if the new management steered the gallery away from its roots in the community and it became some rarefied art box that no-one went to any more or understood. The important thing is its comprehensiveness, its attempt to educate people in the nature of contemporary art – it's a community building and should be accessible."

He wouldn't like any narrowing of the spectrum?

"Not at all. I'd like to be able to walk in and see anything from informed modern painters like Christopher Wood and Dod Proctor to an installation by the latest contemporary worker to a solo exhibition that is the fruition of a career – either from within the region or outside. I'd like to see a national touring show or two – but pretty diverse ones. Chasing the chimera that there is such a thing as 'the avant garde' would not, I think, be the purpose that Passmore Edwards had in mind when he gave the building."

But there must be room for the new stuff?

"Yes, and that's where the funding needs to be. And it's where in recent years we were seriously under-funded. I do resent very much SWA saying 'once again your programme is a bit safe', but once again putting no money or effort into making risk possible – you must have the resources to do it. Once you take money from any organisation, public or private, you're in their hands. They determine the way you have to go ...

"There's no such thing as a completely free lunch. Not at all. What one has to do is to steer a clear path to what you want. There are times when you have to say to a heavy-handed patron, 'Hands off – this is our society, our community' and other times when you have to say to your community, 'Hang on, you're getting a bit insular, closed and cliquey. That's the role of an Arts Organiser – to find the balance."

Russell Hedges

Mike Venning (February 1987)

When Russ Hedges went for an interview to Chelsea Art College, he was surprised by the effect his paintings had on the interviewing panel. They found his work very humorous whereas Russ, who considers himself a rather serious person, hadn't ever noted himself cracking up over his paintings/ Nevertheless, reflection on this sent him delving deeper into the multiplicity of layers that exist in his, or any, art.

This provoked the realisation of another seeming paradox. His constant interest has been the English landscape, yet wherever he has lived, the landscape he has painted there has been that of a different part of the country. When living in Norfolk, he painted the Cornish coast and now that he's in Cornwall, the landscape in his pictures is the Buckinghamshire countryside of his childhood.

But Russ's interest in the landscape is not that of the impressionists or any other artistic creed that aims at capturing the fleeting moment. He is interested in images of landscape as well, of Gainsborough and Turner, or the seemingly unconnected non-representational work of modern Americans such as Rothko or Guston. The English landscape tradition is particularly fascinating to him not only for its recording of the changing face of the land, but also for the changing attitudes of the people who own it or live in it.

The succession of veils that the changing land draws across its past is rather like a narrative, or the succession of stage sets during a play. Russ makes the theatrical analogy while emphasising that what he paints cannot be expressed in words. He is most definitely not telling a story in his pictures. The recent paintings hint at the history of the land. The Buckinghamshire village with its air of immaculate tranquillity will no doubt have a war memorial—evidence of relatively recent anguish and immense sadness. Peaceful fields may hide both the past horrors of the black death and the past pleasures of a favoured spot for local lovers.

Now I've begun to give the impression of a painter of representational images. Not so, most of Russ's paintings seem abstract at first glance and only through continued looking do the figurative elements reveal themselves. The pictures mirror the landscape in this respect and the analogy can be extended to the use of paint where swathes of impasto almost obliterate earlier thin washes and staining. Gestural paint strokes mingle with illusionistic techniques to continue this emphasis.

Russ Hedges aims at a synthesis of images, emotions and thoughts, often disparate and full of contradictions and non-sequiturs. Humour intrudes on seriousness just like the garden gnome in the shrubbery or the inevitable discovery of a rusting, abandoned car in the middle of any uninhabited part of Cornwall. Drama is there too, and he remembers with delight the comment on a painting ..... "rather like Macbeth at Crowlas". And the irony there rounds on itself with the thought that one doesn't actually know that heinous dark-age crimes were not committed at Crowlas.

The fascination of artists with landscape is in the ability of the land around us to tell us about ourselves. The English landscape tradition presents us with probably the richest archive of this material available. Russ uses the archive of his subconscious, he doesn't deal with the specific and therefore allows the spectator recourse to his or her own subconscious for reference points in coming to terms with the work. The fuses set in his paintings are slow burning and, like the unfolding of a dramatic plot, there are twists and turns to be negotiated before the dénouement. Traces along the way, he says, and so we all are. A future generation may marvel over out-of-town shopping centres and motorways just as we find pleasure now in stone circles and stately homes.

John Henderson

Sue Monro (August 1983)

There are many artists who spend hours discussing, analysing and interpreting the content, symbols and hidden meanings in their paintings and others, like John Henderson, who prefer to let the paintings themselves do all the talking. This refreshingly honest approach spares him from much of the stereotyping and jargon that tends to flourish in artistic circles. The subjects in his paintings are drawn from the immediately recognisable country environment in a style that possesses the sort of clarity and fine definition that rules out misinterpretation and gives his work the kind of strong identity that almost renders the art critic redundant.

John's paintings have frequently been described as typical of the photographic realist movement, but I find the narrow confines of this classification do rough justice to his particular talent, justifiable to the extent that he uses his eye like a camera to zoom in on details. Many of his canvasses show a myriad of skilfully rendered organic details, heightened by fine, meticulous brushwork that produces a super-real sharp focus finish ... more often associated with the surrealists, but where Dali drew his inspiration from the subconscious, John paints very much from the real world. Unlike many photo-realists, he doesn't quite free his subjects .from romantic or suggestive interpretation, neither does he present his images with the perceptual anonymity of a documentary photograph so there's none of the harshness or lack of delicacy normally associated with photo-realism. This is more obvious in his recent work, where sharpness and precision are still apparent, but accompanied by a softness that lights on subtle tonal and surface textures ... added to this he uses colour to recede or advance images, creating an illusion of depth behind and projection in front of the canvas which takes him further away from the flat, immodulated photo-realist finish.

One of the best ways to appreciate an artist's work is to see the paintings they have done over a long period ... although many of John's earlier paintings, going back to Falmouth Art School days, are now hanging in private and public collections from Europe to New York, there are stlll enough representative samples of his different phases in his own collection to give a reasonable idea of the general direction his work has taken over the past 20 years. This overall view gives a meaning which transcends the sum of the individual parts and provides a flow and energy which adds up to a whole statement. The one constant statement that spills over from phase to phase is that of sheer enjoyment and vitality plus a profound appreciation and sensitivity towards the subject's life force. Establishing a theme and pursuing it with infinite variations has been the hallmark of many distinguished painters ... it has given him the scope to explore a subject from every angle ... to find unexpected patterns and to stretch the minutaeof the microcosm over a large expanse of canvas. Particles. which usually melt into the whole take on a vitality of their own. His earlier animal paintings, in particular, friesian cows languishing supreme on lush carpets of wind-swept grass and blissfully slumbering pigs are painted with such anatomical accuracy and meticulous brushwork one could be forgiven for reaching out to stroke the canvas. In 1976, John started his quite remarkable haystack series ... ordinary haystacks may not sound like the very essence of artistic inspiration ... well not until you've seen one of John's haystacks. They veritably bristle with crisp golden stalks, contrasted against -the hard black/grey of a rubber tyre or an old brlck dangling on orange twine which is tangled with strips of shiny black polythene.

The horizontal layers of hay bales are broken by the vertical uprights of a ladder. This juxtaposition of different surface textures colours, shapes and lines produces a dynamic visual effect. His more recent water paIntings have a more refined, mysterious, suggestive quality, more subtle but no less powerful ... shimmering pools of water with an almost luminous hazy light dancing on leaves and lilies and the canvases arranged so that they overlap, giving a sense of flow and movement in the water. The thread that links up all his different phases is their extraordinary tactile quality which conveys the immediate sensuality inherent in the natural flow of the environment.

He is without doubt an exceptionally gifted artist who in evolution with his contemporaries has known how to incorporate new influences into a personal style that has been enriched and changed according to his own development and response to the natural world around him.

Photo: John with his daughter, Sonia

Patrick Heron

Mike Sagar Fenton (November 1984)

The road from St Ives to Morvah is a spectacular route, displaying nature at her most beautiful and terrible. There are such roads on the coasts of Scotland and Ireland, but there is little to match it in England or even the rest of Cornwall. It is unusually free of what are known as 'developments' and is left more or less to the devices of nature; and it may seem that this is simply because it is so inhospitable, that nobody wants it. Nothing could be further from the truth. The road actually passes through a battleground, through little skirmishes and major campaigns going back many years. It also passes the house of one of the principal defenders of its wildness, the artist Patrick Heron.

Although he is not aggressive by nature, Heron has a strong, stubborn, tenacious streak which drives him to raise his voice when others are silent. He cannot tolerate the prospect of beauty and vitality being sapped or spoiled by stupidity, ignorance or greed. He cannot suffer fools in positions of power. He is angry about the erosion of freedom, in whatever form it takes. (The mere mention of the present government makes him almost incoherent with frustrated rage.) These passions led him, shortly after the war, to extend his expression from painting to writing, and his writing was often as revolutionary as his painting. He wrote fiery diatribes against the stuffy and pompous world of the post-war Art establishment, and balanced these by his advocacy of little known or under-appreciated artists like Peter Lanyon, Bryan Winter, Roger Hilton, Bernard Leach and Ben Nicholson.

However, in 1960 his attention was suddenly drawn away from the world of international art and focused closer to home, much closer. A plan had been conceived to redevelop some old mine workings on Carnelloe Head (just to the west of Zennor Head). The plans were nothing if not ambitious, involving the supposed employment of 350 men, the building of 100 'cottages', road widening, street lighting from Zennor to Gurnard's Head, etc. etc. Heron was aghast, and plunged immediately into organising opposition to the scheme.

It was a prolonged and difficult business. Tin mining is one of the oldest of Cornish traditions and a popular cause, at least in theory. The prospect of mass employment also has a powerful appeal. The issue split the area and caused a great deal of bitterness and division. In 1960 the words 'environment' and 'ecology' were technical terms, usually found only in biologists textbooks, and the word 'conservationist' had yet to be coined, so Heron was referred to in Penzance council chamber as "That trouble-making Beatnik up at Zennor".

However, the Beatnik had some fairly well-known Beatnik friends, John Betjeman for example, who proceeded to raise a racket that was heard throughout the country. The north coast of West Penwith entered the public consciousness for the first—but definitely not the last—time. Battle was joined; Alan Whicker confronted Heron with Mr Harry, the mine's proponent, on Carnelloe Head for the *Tonight* programme; and a public enquiry met and considered. Although the inspector recommended the scheme, the decision of the Housing Minister was to turn the application down.

This was by no means the end of the affair, which lasted 4½ years from start to finish. The mine's supporters entered a more cautious application, merely to undertake test drillings—they had learnt a lesson from the thrashing some of their more extravagant claims had received in the first enquiry. The opposition had no trouble in seeing through this subterfuge (now universally adopted in such matters, ie the CEGB's 'test drillings' for nuclear power stations) but much more trouble in stopping it, and it was in fact passed by a second public enquiry. Fortunately for the 'Beatnik' lobby, the steam had by then gone out of the mining scheme and their rights were finally curtailed by housing minister Richard Crossman with no further action.

During this time Patrick and Delia Heron's commitment to the protection of the landscape had culminated in their acquisition of 160 acres of moorland around Eagle's Nest, as far as Zennor Quoit. This had been provoked by a plan to buy the farm which owned the moor and turn its buildings into ten holiday letting units. Together with other local farmers, they managed to outwit and outbid the businessmen whose plan it was. They resolved to keep their share of the spoils for the enjoyment of all, and to that end they covenanted it to the National Trust, in which, at that time, they fervently believed.

It wasn't long before the next threat arrived, a threat which still periodically rears its head. The Lords of the Admiralty, having decided to upgrade Culdrose as a major helicopter base, cast around for a suitable patch of open country on which their chaps could practise helicopter manoeuvres and Commando exercises. Their gaze fell upon Zennor moors. Heron discovered quite by chance that they had applied for a 'planning clearance' for 355 acres of moorland for use in training exercises, land which began literally at his front door. When he sought details of the nature of the exercises he was told that they were 'secret'. This was understandably not satisfactory, and by diverse means he discovered that the Admiralty wanted clearance to deploy "Not more than 100 men" and "not more than eight helicopters" for "not more than six consecutive days and nights in any one: month".

Heron blew the gaff in every direction he could think of, including Sir Caspar John, son of Augustus John, who was First Sea Lord at the time. There was instant local outrage and protest; but the Empire struck back. However, Heron and others pressed their attack, publicly proving that the Admiralty's claims of consent were in fact a pack of lies—they actually had consent for less than a quarter of the 355 acres claimed—and in the face of public wrath, the Admiralty staged a strategic withdrawal.

More recently, in 1982, Culdrose applied to land helicopters on Wicca Farm for the purpose of landing and picking up trainees, thus making their training more 'realistic'. The application was couched in the most reasonable terms, but Heron is now an old campaigner and can recognise the thin end of a wedge when he sees one. His opposition was successful, but drew fierce criticism from, of all quarters, the National Trust. Their area representative scolded him for not being willing to "make sacrifices" in the nation's hour of need (shortly after the Falklands debacle). Considering that the Trust were at the time handing over entrusted woodlands to the RAF for a nuclear bunker, and breaking up Treveal Farm at Zennor to sell as a holiday home, Heron's opinion of the Trust fell to absolute zero.

More recently still, he has helped to give wider publicity to the 'stone age bingo' affair, the large white numbers painted on prominent rocks on the moors (obviously for military use) which has been the subject of a long campaign in the *Voice*.

He also finds time, somehow, to paint.

Rose Hilton

Mercia Kemp (July 1987)

Paintings do furnish a room. So do marauding cats, wisps of fog, vases of fresh and dead flowers, battered old hats and decrepit welly boots. People do furnish a room. Rose Hilton's house is a well furnished house and Rose a gracious hostess from whom I learned that you can hold posh dinner parties and set your table with smeared glasses and dubious cutlery and still give your guests more interesting visuals and a better time than if they were dining at the Connaught.

Sitting at the Botallack Hilton with Rose on a foggy summer's morning talking about her painting, the conversation strays to friends and feelings and faraway places, family, holidays past and future and, while we talk, the paintings are there to be looked at, blue and white and blue and red and blue and brown and blue, shapes long and wide and all the blurred, timid personages that populated Rose's canvases are there, but this time they have lost their timidity and they look out in readiness for Rose's command. For she's undoubtedly in control of her art now, no longer tentative, reaping the benefits of years of hard working and living.

Talking about art. She tells me of an exhibition she went to see at the Hayward. 'Munch paints the workers'. "The workers were incidental. The paintings were great." She sees her work that way. She paints what's around her, but her interest is with the way of the paint and the volumes and colours. It is through these that she wants to reach people's sensibilities, the subject matter, charming though it is, is less important to her. She prefers her more ambiguous work to what she calls her "pictorial" paintings. She is happy with her recent exhibition at the Newlyn Orion. We discuss the great value of exhibiting one's work, not just as a show case to the public but as an opportunity for the artist to see a body of work displayed together in sympathetic surroundings and draw conclusions that will promote growth. Also, in Rose's case, the exhibition has been a financial success beyond her wildest dreams, which only goes to show that there are still people with money and taste. More power to her brush.

She wants to paint people dressed up to go to Ascot. "Wonderful shapes and colours" she says. Sitting at the table in Rose's garden, the first of the summer feasts before us, her friends will wear hats and long gowns and look through our binoculars at the passing cows for Rose to have Ascot at her doorstep. Rose's garden—where summer evenings, I swear it, are longer and the art of conversation is alive and well.

Rose's boundless generosity, her tremendous support to other artists, her loving care for her friends, are only too obvious to those who know her. Her extraordinary personality shines out of her paintings. I should like to own one for the pleasure of her company hanging on my wall.

Rose looks at the future with eagerness and optimism. Her children have grown up, her work as keeper and curator of Roger Hilton's paintings looks after itself, thanks to her caring ministrations, and she has rented a studio away from her home at Botallack where she can get on with her painting undisturbed. She feels she's at the threshold of new things and, for the first time she's sure that she has chosen the right way for her painting. "I was always sure that it was there," she says, "but now I can see it."

Plant Food

Patrick Hughes

Martin Val Baker (September 1986)

M.V.B. Where do you come from?
P.H. If I'm asked that I'd answer, from the top end of the working class, or postwar suburbia, or public libraries or the Butler Education Act—not one place, it's more true to say of someone like me that I was a grammar school boy than that I was born in Birmingham.

M.V.B. Did you go to Art School?
P.H. No, I wanted to be a writer and was going to a Training College to specialise in English Literature. The writers I liked at the time were Lewis Carrol, Kafka, Ionesco—the absurdist writers; the college thought that Literature was just the nineteenth century novel, Dickens and George Eliot—the classics. They suggested that I did Art instead and I realised that if you had a certain point of view you could express yourself through art as well as literature. After Training College, I came out and taught for two years at Primary schools and then I was an art teacher at a Secondary Modern for a year.

M.V.B. Did those experiences qualify you for Art School teaching?
P.H. I'd already had my first One-Man show in 1961 when I left college and was working as an artist in my spare time; the Art Schools can employ you as a working artist.

M.V.B. What sort of paintings were you doing at this time?
P.H. I was painting gloss paint on hardboard, things like Liquorice Allsorts and Clothes Pegs—all sorts of imagery, very bright colours.

M.V.B. When did the screen printing start?
P.H. That came much later. If a painting really worked and several people were interested, I would have prints made of it.

M.V.B. Did the buyers of the originals mind at all about the prints?
P.H. No, not usually, there's a lot of bullshit about printmaking, the origins of printing is to enable you to have more than one copy of something. In the Art world they make such a fuss about prints, Marshall McLuhan said that when a technology ceases to be new it becomes a hobby. The ancient forms of warfare, archery and caber tossing persist as hobbies. When the technology is out of date, like etching and screen printing they become artistic techniques. The most laborious and out of date techniques are the most highly favoured in art, whilst the most modern and convenient ones, like coloured Xerox for instance are the least favoured.

M.V.B. Not the end result but the amount of time put in matters?
P.H. And in a way the amount of crudity, an etching can only reproduce easily in one colour and in line, whereas the colour Xerox can reproduce in colours and in many tones. Print making in art is just an element of Luddite snobbery.

M.V.B. When did the Rainbow series start?
P.H. I'd done some in the 'sixties as pictures but the printmaking started about ten years ago, I think I've done about fifty rainbow screen prints and as many again as paintings that were never used as prints. In the Rainbow series I tried to think of all the things a rainbow couldn't do and then do the opposite. Rainbows are usually seen in ones or twos, so I would fill the sky with them; they are always the right way up, so I would do them upside down; they are always coloured, so I would do a grey rainbow; or because they are so large I would put them in a domestic situation.

The idea came gradually; at one point I thought that I could only do so many, some were very difficult to achieve, but after a while I found that I could do them quite easily. I can invent them; I thought at one time that I could only discover them. It's been a problem for me, the rainbows; I'm identified with them, typecast, a lot of my more highbrow friends thought they were too popular.

M.V.B. So you've made a conscious decision to stop them?
P.H. And so have my publishers, the postcard publisher is not interested in rainbows any more, they are looking for something new.

M.V.B. In the present show there are one or two new themes: the eggs, the skeletons and the Yin Yang figures; are you trying to find a substitute rainbow?
P.H. Sort of. You explore to see how many associated ideas you can get out of something. It's like a miner testing a vein to see if it is deep and full and strong; sometimes it is disappointing and you soon exhaust the vein and other times you find that there's more than you expected. I also did a whole load of crucifixes; that was the most poignant, the fullest vein, I surprised myself.

M.V.B. Was that to do with religious feelings?
P.H. Mine are mostly anti-religious feelings, but I suppose one has so many feelings about Christianity and the way it has been used that there are a lot of things you could say about it. So I've made a lot of fun of Christianity, though it's never going to be a very popular vein as anti-religious interest is fairly limited.

M.V.B. You might have difficulty with that. Public Bodies would be wary of hanging them, though you could make political points with the rainbows and get away with it. Do you find it frustrating that some images don't have the colour spectrum of the rainbow?
P.H. Yes, it would be great if there were another image with all the colours; the nearest that some other artists have found is the palette itself.

M.V.B. Your new paintings are water colours.
P.H. Because they are water colours I can do more than I used to. I've been doing three a day—I have a sign in my studio saying 'Three a day'. I work a nine to five day.

M.V.B. I noticed at the show that you had one price for your bigger paintings and another for the smaller ones; do you ever feel so happy with a smaller one that you would charge the price of a larger one?
P.H. The prices don't relate to the aesthetic worth, but that's true generally. A picture by Jasper Johns is not really worth £1 million and by comparison a Roger Hilton is not worth £500: the Hilton should be about £15,000 and the Jasper Johns £5000. The relation between prices is so arbitrary, the idea that you have to price them is daft, so I just put the same prices on them.

M.V.B. What do you see happening in the future?
P.H. I want to use another medium. I'm going to use oils again; I've used watercolours over the last year, I used gloss for twenty years, gouache for three and then acrylic—all very tight. I will follow a new freedom with oils, not bother about finishing off, allow more accidents—I've never allowed an accident.

Bert Jansch

Martin Val Baker (September 1989)

Folk guitarist Bert Jansch, who came to Penzance in August for two sell-out concerts, talked to the Voice at The Acorn about his life as a performer.

Voice: You came from Scotland, are you Scottish?

BJ: Yes, I was born in Glasgow and brought up in Edinburgh.

Voice: In the 'sixties you were involved with Robin Williamson and Clive Palmer in running folk clubs there.

BJ: We used to run the Crown Club in Edinburgh, we ran on a Wednesday and Archie Fisher and his mob did the Tuesday night. There was a lot going on then; we all lived in a squat together.

Voice: Then you moved to London. Had you got a record deal?

BJ: Not then. First I travelled around Europe busking.

Voice: In those days, did you consider yourself more of a guitar player or a songwriter?

BJ: I don't think you consciously thought about that, you just did it. I was writing songs at the time. I was very much into the Bob Dylan 'I want to say something' phase in those days; now I write a song occasionally but I have come back to traditional music more.

Voice: You had quite a following then, working solo and later with John Renbourn. Did you and John do much work as a duo?

BJ: We didn't actually work as a duo; we did two separate shows and then did a bit together at the end

Voice: ... and then Pentangle. How did that come about?

BJ: John and I wanted to start a club where we could experiment with various different musicians, and the band eventually grew out of that. The club was at the Horseshoe, Tottenham Court Road, we ran it for about a year, lots of people came there, Sandy Denny and the Fairport people.

Voice: Was there a lot of cross fertilisation?

BJ: Well it was odd, you'd have the occasional session where Dominic Behan or Doris Henderson or someone would suddenly appear, quite a lively time.

Voice: Were Pentangle successful right from the start?

BJ: We played at the club for about a year and then our first outside gig was at the Royal Festival Hall.

Voice: Pentangle were a little jazz tinged?

BJ: Yes, through Danny Thompson and Terry Cox.

Voice: How would you classify yourself?

BJ: I suppose as a folk singer, because I tend to sing traditional folk music—a bit of blues perhaps.

Voice: Are you continually arranging new songs? Does your set change a lot over a year?

BJ: It constantly changes. I usually have a new project on the go. At the moment it's an album of Celtic songs for Run River Records with Peter Kirtley, it should be out in the spring.

Voice: The songs will all be arranged by you?

BJ: Yes, though there will be lots of other people on it, Maggie Boyle and Steve Tilson among others.

Voice Do you like the idea of guitar players working together, like the Kicking Mule concerts?

BJ: Not really. I think you should shape an evening by the music not by the nature of the instrument. 'A Guitar Night' to me is boring. Mind you, I did a Guitar Night at the Royal Festival Hall with Paco Peña, Jimi Hendrix, myself and Tim Walker, a classical guitar player; that was a good night. But generally it's like going to a 'Night of Clarinet Players'!

Voice: You'd get the guitar nuts up front watching the fingers. Would you like to work with, say, a poet, a jazz pianist, a chamber group, would there be more stimulation?

BJ: Yes. I think a concert like tonight's works because the sort of people who come to see me will enjoy Roger Brooks (the support act) as well.

Voice: How do you see the future, do you enjoy playing solo, duos—could you see another group situation?

BJ: Well, Jacqui McShee and I still run Pentangle and if we're offered a tour for the band we fancy doing, we'll do it.

Voice: You work with Jacqui with Pentangle, with Peter Kirtley, with Nigel Smith, and solo gigs?

BJ: I very rarely work solo, though I go to the States this October on a solo tour for the first time I'm a bit scared of it! Mitch Greenhill is organising it so it should be OK. I get occasional work in Europe. I'm always glad to hear of bookings in any combination

Voice: Are you writing any new stuff at the moment?

BJ: I come up with a song now and again. I've got one at the moment called *The Parting* which is just an idea of friends flowing away for good. Peter and I are doing a session for Gordon Giltrap, who's organising an album featuring various people playing instruments by guitar-maker Bob Armstrong.

Voice: What about Modern Music, the World Music boom, have you any interest in that?

BJ: Music is always a good thing!

Voice: Do you go out and listen when you have the time?

BJ: Not unless I'm really pulled! Maybe if a favourite of mine is in town I'll make a special effort, like Derrol Adams. There's a lot of good music about, there always will be.

Voice: But basically your main interest would be British traditional music rather than other countries' music, or crossover experiments like Danny Thompson's.

BJ: Yes, I'm still locked into the British side of things!

Wizz Jones

Martin Val Baker (June 1989).

Guitarist and singer Wizz Jones seems to have been around forever. A major influence on a generation of British guitar players, he first turned up in these parts in the summer of 1959 on the recommendation of fellow musician Malcolm (Woody) Price who had worked in Cornwall the previous season. Wizz remembers busking on the beaches around Newquay as one of the bohemian/beatnik influx of those days and was featured in a TV programme on the 'problem' made by Alan Whicker and the *Tonight* team.

Wizz and Malcolm Price were part of a group of London teenagers who based themselves around the Soho coffee bars, playing skiffle and American folk music, having been impressed by the performances of visiting Americans. Big Bill Broonzy (whose influence on Wizz still shows), Rambling Jack Elliot, Derroll Adams and Guy Carawan were all guests at the club run by bluesman Alexis Korner. Inspired by the gypsy lifestyle of the Americans, Wizz and his contemporaries travelled to Paris, "there was a wonderful guitar player there called Geno Foreman who really turned Davey Graham on," and then to the French Riviera. Wizz had been playing with Davey Graham and Long John Baldry in the streets of London, and in France he teamed up with Clive Palmer and Mick Softly. At that time there was the beginning of the English rock scene in London with Tommy Steele, Cliff Richard and the Shadows attracting a lot of attention, but "we were pretty disdainful about all that, we didn't mix with them, we were alternative!"

Although Wizz had earned money in various clubs playing C&W and skiffle, his first paid gig on the developing folk circuit was in Yorkshire as a support to Steve Benbow. As the folk boom progressed Wizz formed a duo with banjo player Pete Stanley, getting "loads of work" around the circuit, with regular summer seasons in Cornwall where, as well as hotel gigs, they became the main attraction at the newly opened Folk Cottage at Mitchell. The Folk Cottage in its heyday ran several nights a week (often with all night sessions) featuring the likes of Ralph McTell, Pete Berryman, Clive Palmer, Michael Chapman *et al* and had a significant influence on the local Cornish music scene.

After splitting with Pete Stanley, Wizz worked for a while in London with Clive Palmer who had just left the Incredible String Band, and they recorded an LP for Pete Eden that was never released "a very obscure Clive-type album; he was playing some lovely stuff." In 1969, Wizz first went to Germany and over the following decade developed quite a following there through club and festival appearances, recording LPs both as a solo performer and with his group Lazy Farmer. The group was formed in 1973 when Wizz felt his solo work was drying up a little, and comprised of his wife Sandy, Don Cogging and two well known Cornish musicians, John Bidwell and Jake Walton. Lazy Farmer toured Europe (where Wizz now had a manager) several times, promoting their album which had been released on a German label, and "actually made money!"

For a long time Wizz Jones has been associated with the haunting songs of Alan Tunbridge, an artist who had travelled with him in the early Newquay days. "He produced some beautiful songs and I have been a real champion of them throughout my career, though I think it may have limited my own song writing." Recently Tunbridge moved to Australia and Wizz has been adapting and arranging songs by other people, "I'm always on the lookout for new material though for every dozen I start on only one or two actually work." In fact Wizz is an extremely adept arranger of other people's songs (listen to his version of Robin Williamson's *The First Girl I Loved*) and the breadth of his material astounding. His present set includes a Stevie Wonder number and he is working on a Tom Robinson song at the moment.

Just recently Ian Anderson re-released the compilation LP *Matchbox Days* which included one of Wizz's numbers, and this stirred up some interest in the media so perhaps the British folkies are entering the nostalgia period at last. Wizz has also recorded with Derroll Adams and there is an unreleased tape with Jack Elliot that he is particularly proud of. His present ambition is to record an album with his son Simmy who plays sax as a session musician, and also with a number of well known bands in London.

Over the years Wizz has made several LPs; the first through Chas McDevitt's enthusiasm was for Columbia with Pete Stanley and then with John Renbourn for CBS, followed by a couple for Ian Anderson's Village Thing label as well as the German releases. The recording Wizz feels most happy with is *Happiness was Free* on the German label Intercord. "Pete Berryman plays wonderful guitar on it; the other albums have their moments but as far as I'm concerned it's the best thing I ever did—it's the only one I can play right through and say, yes, that's what I'm about. We had total freedom in the studio, the LP was deleted long ago but one day I hope to buy the tapes and re-release it as a double album with the best of the Village Thing recordings."

Although Wizz expresses real terror at the thought of concert performance, and says he prefers the intimacy of club sessions, he has in the past produced impressive shows (notably locally at St Ives Guildhall) to a concert audience. In 1972, he travelled as support to Pentangle's last British tour, culminating in a concert at the Royal Festival Hall, and he also supported a ten gig tour by John Martyn with Paul Kossof and Danny Thompson, though he felt a little out of his depth with the 'Rock 'n Roll' lifestyle.

Over the years Wizz has lived in a fairly moderate fashion, avoiding the over-indulgences of some of his contemporaries; his growing family has always been important to him, and for years they would all pile into a battered old Volkswagen van and cross Europe in search of the next gig. Fortunately as his reputation spread Wizz found it easier to get work in obscure corners of Europe in the boom years of the 'seventies. However, as the economic recession of the 'eighties began to bite, first the British and then the European audiences abandoned acoustic music and by 1985 Wizz found himself back on the dole.

For the last four years Wizz has worked as a furniture van driver with gigs interspersed on a part-time basis, but the rising interest in acoustic music promises well for the future, and he now feels his appetite for playing returning. The only problem he has is on the marketing side, his music, "is not a saleable product, it's too confusing, not blues, not original, a bit of everything, you can't market that; it's never a problem with the audience, they seem to like it, but you can't convince the middleman that it's saleable. I'm not griping, that's the way it is."

WILKO
JOHNSON
AFRICA

Suzanne Juta

Martin Val Baker (April 1985)

Suzanne Juta has her first major exhibition, at the Salt House Gallery, St Ives, this month (16th April-8th May), in combination with the Newlyn potter Alan Brough. Suzanne's unusual collages are created entirely from hand made paper, with some 'found objects' and paint added occasionally. The paper is made from plants such as bamboo, banana leaves, daffodils, bluebells, bracken and wild garlic, in fact any plant with a fibrous texture can be used. The plants are cut into small pieces and boiled in caustic soda, and then, after washing out the soda, pulped with a stone. After blending in a domestic mixer, the mixture is poured into a tank of water into which is dipped a framed mesh on the surface of which the paper is formed as the water drains away. Often Suzanne will insert threads, pine needles, leaves, photos or bits of print to give an added texture, often causing unexpected results, as the effect on the final colour cannot be absolutely predicted. The resulting paper, which is mainly of a warm browny-gold hue, is added to the hoard of materials built up over the years and from which she builds up her collages. Rather than having a planned image, Suzanne likes to improvise, with an image and title eventually suggesting itself and being more defined by the addition of a little paint. Titles such as: Osiris Rising, Woman and Snake, Black Moon Silver Moon, reflect her favourite re-occurring themes with mythological, oriental, seasonal and local influences evident. The finished works are box mounted behind glass, with large white borders giving them room to breathe.

Suzanne Juta came to Cornwall from Leeds in 1981 (though originally from London). She studied briefly at Falmouth Art School and then gained a Fine Arts degree at Leeds University. Following a Teacher Training Course she taught Art and French, later working as a Community Artist in Yorkshire for two years. In 1976 she learned the paper making process and experimented with unusual plants to explore the technique's full potential. Though originally working in abstract forms she has more recently found a figurative element emerging. The St Ives show will feature 30-40 of Suzanne's pieces and next term she will be teaching paper making at Falmouth Art School. Although this is her first major show, she has exhibited in mixed shows at the Penwith, Newlyn, Falmouth and Salt House Galleries since leaving full time teaching to concentrate on her paper work.

Silvia Kantaris

Dave Scott (October 1991)

An interview commencing with a generous glass of red wine is condemned to certain disorder, a conversational rather than inquisitive level.

After half an hour of such instructively entertaining discussion, we all three appeared suddenly to wake up. "When," inquired Silvia, "is the interview going to begin?"

"It has," we replied from behind the second—or was it the third—glass each. And so it went on.

"One would think—looking at the list of Laureates— that more men than women are poets."

"In fact, it's the other way about, but not many women poets get published. I started my career in Australia, where it's easier for a poet to become known. Back in England, I had to start all over again."

"Why Cornwall?"

"How prosaic—no particular reason, my husband's job initially; a sympathy that developed steadily."

Raised from native stock in Derbyshire's Peak District, some of her most moving poems touch the figurescapes of a crowded childhood in a two-roomed house among a large family "where slop wouldn't wash."

"No mod cons?"

"No cons at all."

"Yeats?"

"A favourite—you heard about the Monkey Glands?"

"What did Maud Gonne think of them?"

"She doesn't seem to have said a lot."

"How discreet. You wanted to write from an early age?"

"Let me modestly flaunt this old school exercise-book." Tidy handwriting was compulsory in those days; a balance in the phrasing and density of texture reveals youthful promise. "Let's say I knew what I was from around that time."

"And the next collection?"

"I make no secret of this." A newspaper cutting baldly records an attempted strangulation, a conviction for assault, a paltry fine.

"An affair?"

"Three years of it—written *in situ*."

"You think the poetic temperament more prone to trouble in that arena?"

"Can we leave that question open—there's no lack of evidence if you care to look for it."

Our interview keeps hovering on the edge of a writer's collaboration; after all, what further baring of the soul can be demanded of a poet than should be already in the work. If it is not, we are looking at not poetry but masquerade.

"The function of poetry?"

"Well, there are many—but, chiefly, sedition."

"You have a reputation as a daring poet."

"And as a collaborator—doesn't that sound wicked?"

News from the Front (1983), a collection on a common theme, cooperatively composed with D M Thomas, is both daring and seditious, more than faintly disturbing often quite brutal, in places touchingly funny. On a more ethereal level, a joint project with Philip Grosse *The Air Mines of Mistila* (I admit I have only dipped into it) is more quirky, more fun, more inspiringly inventive. All artists develop—"And poets are no exception."

Something is ironic about the situation. The house, tucked away cosily enough, is no Cornish granite cottage. The only overt eccentricity is a companionless gatepost doing service as a Menhir on the front lawn.

"There's comfort in respectable surroundings."

"I've heard that referred to as the aspidistra principle."

"That I like."

"Hermann Hesse made the same point in *Steppenwolf*."

As well as being a highly regarded poet (one of the few making an actual living at it), and the holder of an MA and two Ph.Ds, Silvia (as she would prefer to be spelt) is quite free of the preciousness attendant on success. Tea-break is the fourth (or is it the sixth?) glass of red wine followed by a quick tinkle on the Bechstein: "I don't play myself—of course, I wish I did."

With something of an effort, some sort of track is regained.

"Robert Frost?"

"A widely imitated poet—original poets do get imitated. Closer to home, Peter Redgrove is another who comes to mind."

At normal interviews, the subject, by signals subtle or otherwise, indicates the finale. This time, it is we who are feeling the strain.

"What can we finish with?"

"Something we all like."

"A Cornish saying?"

"When the Gorse is out of bloom, then kissing's out of fashion."

"And, perhaps, we'll see you later down the pub."

Ida Kelarova

Carole Bishop (April 1990)

The exotic gypsy singer, who returned for the third time to Penwith last month, talked to Carole Bishop for the Voice about her life.

I was born in North Moravia, Czechoslovakia. My father was a very talented musician but because he was a gypsy he didn't have much work. My mother, who was a teacher, pushed him and he became one of the best musicians in the country, playing traditional and classical music (double bass).

Czechoslovakia is very racist they really think gypsies should be hanged—so he pretended to be Czechoslovakian and denied his gypsy roots.

We travelled a lot in the early days but eventually settled in the capital of Moravia. However, he would often take me back to his village. Sometimes I'd wake up in the night and hear them all outside playing their music, my father with tears running down his face. They were all musical. It was then that I heard the songs which my father never played to me, they were very secret. I had to hide and listen, if they saw me they'd stop playing.

One day when I was seven, an uncle at the village told me we were gypsies. I had no idea. My family went mad and denied it, but I gradually realised it was true. When I was 25, my grandmother lost her memory; then she suddenly started speaking gypsy; I'd never heard it before. That shocked me and I realised the depth of the culture. They all told her to shut up. It was so secret we were never able to talk about it.

I have very happy memories of my father's village. Life was very simple; it was very special, like a dream. My father always went back he was really himself there.

I've studied music since the age of six—my father encouraged us. Every town has its own music school. Penzance would have one for example. I was studying classical music, piano, cello and drama. Later, I went to the conservatoire, then to the academy. I was 25 when I finished. I was invited to join one of the best theatres in Czechoslovakia, the Divadlo na Provasku, and I was with them for six years. I was very successful and making a good living. We travelled quite a lot and in 1983 went to the Festival of Fools in Copenhagen where I met my husband to be, Tony, who is English. We couldn't speak each other's language but we fell in love. The whole festival organised the wedding—150 people came from all over the world.

I wanted to live in Czechoslovakia because I had everything there; a house, a good career, but the communists decided to punish me because I married without permission. There was a scandal and they didn't recognise the wedding, but they wouldn't let us marry as Tony's papers showed he already was married—to me, of course!

It took three months to sort out. I had to write letters of apology etc. But even then they treated Tony like a tourist and made him change £9 a day. Eventually he ran out of money so we decided to leave. I had to buy his ticket with dollars (bought at great expense on the black market). I became very bitter with my country at this point and decided I'd had enough. I'd make my home in England.

We moved to Pembrokeshire to find a house. I had to start from scratch—I couldn't even speak the language. The first year and a half was quite depressing. Something was missing and I didn't know what it was. We moved to Denmark but things were the same there to start with. Then I went to Christiania, which reminded me of the village at home. My father had died and I thought, "All I have left is the songs." So I decided to give a workshop and performance and it all started there.

Before long I was teaching from nine to nine and travelling all round the country. But I started doing more than just teaching them the songs. I'd say, "Come on, couldn't you feel it?" I found out they couldn't sing the songs so I questioned what is behind the voice. Out of that came the kind of work I do now which gives people the opportunity to express themselves in a very honest way. It wakes up some of the passions people have and can release years of pain which they haven't allowed themselves to show in their lives. There is incredible power in every person.

I've been teaching and performing around Europe—Denmark and Norway regularly, and this year Germany, Holland, Italy, and soon I am going to the Orkneys.

In Denmark, there is a group of people I have been working with for many years—eight singers and four musicians. We perform a whole concert together and are very successful there. I'd love to bring them here but it would cost too much. In 1986 I went back to Czechoslovakia performing underground. Six hundred people came and it was great but I don't want to live there again; my home is here now. I live close to Chester with Tony, my son from a previous marriage, who's fifteen now, and our daughter of five.

For the future, I'd like to set up a group to work with regularly like I have in Denmark. Also I have done a project in Denmark where we had five teachers—from Zimbabwe, the Caribbean, England and France and we all taught our techniques in the same workshop. I'd like to do something like that here, too. I'd rather work here in Cornwall than in London.

David Kemp

Martin Val Baker (November 1985)

"I don't like answering questions," he said, before I could get one in. This could be a difficult assignment.

David Kemp lives just off the coast road between Pendeen and St. Just in a little cottage on the side of a hill. Further up the slope is his studio/workshop, at present denuded of his best work which is on exhibition at the Manchester City Art Gallery. A Londoner, he came to Cornwall thirteen years ago, after spells in the Merchant Navy and at Farnham and Wimbledon Art Schools. At first, Kemp worked as a painter, and his rounded landscapes and decorated furniture were familiar sights in the local galleries. In the mid-seventies, he moved to Crean, near St. Buryan, and it was whilst using a nearby cowshed as a studio that he began to notice old bits of abandoned agricultural machinery lying around. Piecing some of them together, he produced his first assemblage, a pre-historic winged monster on wheels that he entitled 'The Chariot'. Since then, Kemp has become a magpie, a collector of Cornwall's industrial waste, (though perhaps the comparison should be with a seagull), a scavenger who puts to good use the unwanted and worn out remains of a past industrial era. Countless forays over agricultural and mining sites, as well as car dumps and even domestic rubbish tips have produced a wealth of raw materials that seem to have been ignored by other artists in the area. I was reminded of St. Ives wood sculptor, Max Barret's incredulity that earlier artists had not seen the possibilities of the wooden remains of the town's decaying 'New' quay. However, since the recent filling in of some of Kemp's favourite sites, he has taken to a bit of beachcombing himself.

From his vast collection, Kemp has assembled a veritable Noah's Ark of unusual creatures, birds, animals and humanoid figures, relics, he claims, from the last Machine Age, and indeed one could easily imagine the pieces being unearthed at some futuristic archaeological dig. Kemp insists that he is a populist in art terms and that his assemblages are intended to be easily recognisable, understandable and above all, humorous. It is perhaps this latter concept that tends to make some of the more serious artistic interests a little wary of him, and thus Kemp himself, a little wary of them. The surreal effect of his works are enhanced particularly when they are placed in relevant surroundings, for example, tin monsters scavenging amongst derelict tin mines, a 'Mock Turtle' gambols at the sea's edge and his 'Iron Horse' languishes on one of Newcastle's metro stations.

More and more of Kemp's work is exhibited out of the county. As well as participation in several touring Arts Council collections, he has had a number of solo exhibitions, notably at Wigan, Sheffield, Swansea, Exeter and Manchester. In 1981, he was invited to be resident sculptor at Grisedale Forest Cumbria (jointly sponsored by the Northern Arts and the Forestry Commission) and returned there in '82 and '84. It was here that he created his 'Birdman's Hat', an eccentric Red Indian-like structure in a forest clearing (built entirely from forest off-cuts and refuse) as a sanctuary for the occasional bird. or walker who frequents this remote spot. Further residences followed, at Newcastle, Margam Park in Wales (where he built the strangely threatening 'Conocydd Drews'—subtitled 'A misguided missile') and the Yorkshire Sculpture Park at Bretton Hall. A little flock of his birds adorns the newly-built Liverpool Garden Centre, and Kemp feels that this once again reflects the much greater civic interest in the arts shown by the northern authorities—could you imagine our local councils commissioning work from any of the many artists living in the area!

It is very difficult with words to describe the astonishing array of figures that I had the good fortune to see in slide form—his Manchester show alone featured 98 pieces ranging in size from 15 inches to 15 feet. As Kemp himself says, "I can only explain where I'm at by the things that I make." It seems that it is only the north who are getting that explanation, surely the time has come for a major Kemp show to be staged locally. In the meantime, a lecture with slides would not go amiss—though rather like the visits to country houses of Victorian rake Frank Harris, David Kemp has never lectured in the same place twice! At last I managed to put one of the many difficult questions I had prepared for this story, "What is your favourite colour?" I demanded. "Pink," replied his wife.

Robert Lenkiewicz

Ashley Peters (July 1988)

Robert Lenkiewicz was born in London in 1942, his parents Russian Jewish refugees from the holocaust. He started painting at the age of 9. He saw Charles Laughton playing Rembrandt on TV and that did it . . .

In his personal library of some 70,000 books, 300 of them are on Rembrandt and, in pride of place among them, is the tape of Laughton.

By 15 years old he'd done a massive painting, 364ft x 17ft, in sections, sewn together. It got him into St Martin's School of Art. On to the Royal Academy at 19, working obsessively on a very large scale. It never occurred to him that life was to be lived in any other way. Life was translated through one's creative processes and that was what rendered it significant.

After two enjoyable years at the Royal Academy he was expelled; he's not really sure why. He was married by now, living in Hampstead and had a large studio which he filled with vagrants, drug addicts and social inadequates, and was finally asked to leave by the police.

He moved to Gunnislake to teach for a year, and then on to a flat in Plymouth where history repeated itself. He found large premises, barns etc, filled them with vagrants and painted them. It was a rough and stimulating lifestyle.

Working on a massive scale once more, the first project of his Relationship Series began—Vagrancy, which produced 500 paintings. Since then he has carried out a different project every year, all of them heavily researched. A keen philosopher, his projects are all related to what he calls an aesthetic theory and he takes this aspect of his work very seriously. He keeps copious notes and drawings of his reactions to any event whether folding his trousers, reading Plato, making love or walking across the moor. In a sense he sees some aspects of his enquiry as 'scientific'. He believes that in the future there will be a more serious interest in the whole area of aesthetics from a physiological viewpoint. He feels we just do not know enough about the structure of the brain and our physiology at present. In 50 years time, this aspect of his work may be of use.

Lenkiewicz: "I am interested in what causes physiological sensations. There are obvious interpretations of these things, but I think when we become addicted to somebody (which we designate as the love experience), when we become obsessive about an idea, there is a physiological consequence of an attraction to that idea or that person. In exactly the same way as an heroin addict becomes dependent upon the heroin, or the alcoholic is deprived without any alcohol, so the lover would feel physiological deprivation from the source of his addiction. My claim is that we are not actually concerned about the welfare of that person independently of one's own needs, which is the usual claim of the love experience. We are not concerned at all. All we are concerned about is to voraciously feed our physiological needs. If she orgasms in a particular way or has a certain shape of mouth, breasts, bum or whatever, this is a package that can addict profoundly and when we suffer withdrawal symptoms, they are extremely interesting to study. Hence, the whole project on Jealousy, Love and Romance, Orgasm, Old Age, Death and this project on Education. They are all linked to considerations about the way we become attached to ideas, objects and people and are an attempt to study that physiological process.

"Philosophers, doctors etc, can see that there are grave limitations in our perceptions of concepts like time. Processes in which we interpret the experience of space may all be bound up with it. Our own emotional reaction to almost every event in our lives—what exactly is the emotional process, the chemistry involved and in what way does it relate to aesthetics? Why is taste so profound on every level?"

Lenkiewicz is prolific: There are 10,000 paintings stored around Plymouth he says. He considers the whole of the project is the painting not one single painting. They are rich in hue, the flesh parts in particular. He likes his images to be as loaded as possible. They are full of irony. He sees himself as a presenter of information, arguing that there has never been a time when more information has been available and less used.

And so to section 17 of the Relationship Series—Education.

Lenkiewicz: "I have frequently returned to a single and overwhelming speculation; the nature of the relationship between the Adult and the Child. Education, despite all grandiose schemes, bureaucratic generalisations and cross-referential subtleties, is about this relationship. Education as we experience it in 'civilised' societies is primarily concerned with the linking of human behaviour to commercial enterprise. I consider the dominant feature of education to be the mass commercial exploitation of the young. The history of human slavery is evidence of our capacity to feel no value other than commercial value for other human beings. Our treatment of the young is still characterised by this lack of value. We speak of the young person as 'the future', 'the destiny of mankind' a 'spiritual investment.' Such designations are sentimental and ruthless formulas concealing the slavery referred to.

"Parenthood, as we know it in the western world, experiences the child as property; and this process of preferential treatment is certainly antisocial. An explorer of the Amazon asked a young boy to point out his father. The boy slapped the man's face and with offended passion said, 'I belong to no-one. At this moment you are my father.'

"Education can only be about the noblest of human skills. That skill is the ability to render one's own life significant to oneself without becoming too much of a public nuisance. Adults rarely feel that their lives are significant, and many of these adults are parents.

"The young person's sensitivity to example is immeasurable. A parent or mentor whose creative life is passionless, dulled and uninspired, will have great difficulty in valuing themselves. To de-value oneself is to de-value others. We do not value other people by feeling superior or inferior to them. That is the straight road to Fascism. We know and recognise those moments when our lives feel more enriched and when we feel our sensitivities heightened.

"Nature, human relationships and the arts are our only defence against the unspeakable terror of individual isolation in the scheme of things. Education is about that rare skill, the ability to feel that life is its own reward. We carry our childness like a knapsack for the whole journey of our lives and disrespect for the young reflects clearly the loss of respect for oneself.

"I barely recollect a moment's depression in my life, and I am certainly of an optimistic nature. The projects that I work on are academic surveys of aspects of human behaviour. They attempt to assimilate information impartially. Of the 17 large projects that I have worked on in recent years, this one on the theme of education has been the least salutary and the most sinister and depressing."

The Family is the next section.

The next project: Session
OBSERVATIONS ON LIGHT
EDUCATION.
Opens — APRIL 14 1988
800 sitters have been
involved in the large

Scott Lowndes

Sue Monro (February 1983)

Take a sad, forlorn Meissen figurine minus head and arms, many hours of meticulous work in the competent hands of a skilled porcelain restorer and PRESTO a near miraculous transformation takes place. Even her exquisite dainty fingers and the subtle glow on her rosy cheeks have returned. .. and not a crack or join to be seen anywhere!

Scott Lowndes has been restoring porcelain for 6 years. He works alone in a small shed at the back of his Carnyorth cottage, surrounded by a dazzling array of plates, figures, vases, miniatures, etc, some complete and others in various stages of repair. His interest in restoration was initially stimulated by a friend in Manchester who had 15 years experience in the trade and occasionally showed Scott some examples of his work. Scott was so impressed with the before and after transformations, he talked him into employing him on a two year apprenticeship basis. There is no formal training available for this career, much of what Scott has learned has been through trial, error, self-criticism, experimenting with different techniques and materials and gradually refining the traditional methods. On the day I visited him he was restoring a superb Sèvres Vase and experimenting with Gold Leaf to achieve a perfect match with the original. Gold is the most difficult finish to match.

Different Techniques

There are many different methods of ceramic restoration – often the individual piece will dictate the method. A missing handle or arm would have to be completely remade, taxing the restorers' skills to the utmost. Scott finds these jobs amongst the more rewarding and challenging, if time-consuming, often requiring research via books, prints, old photographs and his own sketches... just to get that 'new head' to match perfectly with the original. Museum repairs rely on bleach cleaning, softer glue and self-coloured filler to minimise the repair but not to hide it. Scott occasionally uses this technique but mostly prefers the total restoration method, where the joins, cracks and remodelled parts are virtually undetectable.

The Tools of The Trade

The basic tools of his trade include araldite for bonding, epoxy fillers, scalpel, an old dentist's drill for shaping and sculpturing, plus various hand-made tools, usually shaped from old saw blades, an air-brush for colour matching and a converted clothes dryer for setting low-temperature enamel glazes. He mixes all his own colours (mostly stove enamels); indeed a good eye for colour along with technical expertise and infinite patience are vital ingredients for success in this trade. He admits to having the occasional jinxed vase that refuses to be restored, glues that inexplicably refuse to set, glazes that bubble and pots that fight him every step of the way... one vast Chinese umbrella vase that came to grief on the kitchen floor only minutes after completion. Fortunately these happenings are rare. Each ceramic has its own identity and individual personality, manufacturer's marks, thumbprints in the glaze, the inspiration of the original craftsmen and the history of the previous owner ... all go to make this a fascinating, absorbing trade.

Making a Living

Inevitably Scott faces many of the dilemmas and difficulties experienced by self-employed people: financial insecurity, the self discipline required for long hours working alone surrounded by homelife and family distractions. Most of his work comes via Antique shops but on the whole he finds private commissions more satisfying simply because the customer has so much more interest in the piece being restored. Scott recommends to anyone wishing to do their own repairs not to use Araldite ... Bostik is preferable as it's softer and badly-positioned joins can be reset.

So if you have a box of broken treasures in the attic or a favourite piece of china crying out to be restored to its former glory, contact Scott on 787287 for a free quotation.

Benjamin Luxon

Mike Venning (June 1986)

Benjamin Luxon is someone at the top of a sophisticated profession which has taken him all over the world, yet he still retains his Cornishness. This is not a paradox, although we are often inclined to accept a scenario that divides the Cornish into those who leave and only return for sentimental reasons, and those who stay put and become inward-looking, slightly xenophobic even. It ain't necessarily so, and Benjamin is realistically in touch with his roots and the wider world. He recently became president of the Cornwall Arts Centre Trust, which is working to provide a purpose-built theatre and arts centre for Cornwall to be situated in Truro. This is not just a figurehead role and he is involved in canvassing the county council as well as providing his own knowledge and expertise and that of his contacts in the theatre and opera world to ensure the best possible facilities for such a centre.

Born in Redruth because that's where the hospital was, he is a Camborne man in fact. He sang throughout his childhood (his family was musical in the Cornish sense—bands, choirs and chapel). He went to Truro School and on to Westminster College to train as a P.E. teacher. Singing was always a vital part of his life, but he hadn't thought of it as a career or vocation . While at college his potential was first recognised by a visiting opera singer who was impressed enough to suggest that he got his voice trained. His reply was "How?" She suggested the Guildhall School of Music. He went along, was accepted and the real business of a singing career began.

Awareness of the quality of his voice and the possibility of making singing his life was dawning and he began to tailor his work (he was a P.E. teacher by now) to fit in with this new vocation. He has a baritone voice and has always been an all-rounder, able to sing a wide spectrum of styles rather than concentrating on a single area. While still feeling somewhat naïve and unsure of himself in the cultural climate of English classical singing, he succeeded in some of the most sophisticated areas of vocal music. He found himself adept at Baroque and modern works, much of which was broadcast on Radio 3.

Lieder was another happy discovery. At the Guildhall School of Music one teacher was a renowned authority on Lieder and instead of setting practice work of scales, he would present pupils with Lieder songs to work on. Benjamin reckons that this not only gave him a love of Lieder but kept him singing as he feels that nothing but scales would have bored him to death. And he says, all the German composers have produced fantastic songs and he has recorded-a great many of them.

He joined the English Opera Group under the leadership of Benjamin Britten, who Luxon considers the greatest all-round musician he has encountered, brilliant in all fields—composer, conductor and player. Benjamin Luxon's major achievement with this group was the creation of the character Owen Wingrave in Britten's T.V. opera of 1970. Since then he has made his mark in other major roles, notably Eugene Onegin. He has been associated with Glyndebourne, Covent Garden and Frankfurt, and is now an artiste of international renown.

The only area that he hasn't fully explored has been grand opera. The problem is the vocal training. The great operatic roles require amazing sustained power which needs specialist voice training. However this training actually makes it difficult to sing anything but opera and Benjamin wants to be able to continue covering all musical styles and genres. Yet he hasn't avoided grand opera entirely; he enjoys acting and in operatic terms he considers himself an actor-singer as opposed to a singer-actor. He has sung in most of the world's great opera houses with the culmination coming in the near future when he performs at La Scala, something which, even with his wealth of experience, scares him.

Singing is Benjamin Luxon's life. On stage he is totally immersed in both the essence of the music and the total synthesis of physical and mental energy that is the singing voice in full flow. His physical presence while performing is remarkable; he seems to grow in stature when the music swells and soars, and his face and whole body express every nuance of meaning in the words being sung.

The singer is an artist whose acts of creation happen in public view and to see someone completely involved in their art is a mesmeric experience. The performer, too, is entranced by the activity. Singing, Benjamin says, comes not only from tongue or throat, but from the abdomen. Even more, when everything is going right, the force seems to come up from the ground through his legs and filling his whole body. This may not .always happen, but occurs, as he puts "when it works." This is the magic of all art, the painter or poet has the same experience; you know when something works, but not necessarily how or why, it just does and that's the moment for which Benjamin Luxon is constantly searching.

The human body alone is the medium through which singing is created. There are no external accessories; no instruments, no paint, canvas, pen or paper. The raw material is the vital essence of life, breath. This Benjamin suspects, is an almost magical element in the process of singing. People not only listen to the voice but are actually captivated by the singer's mastery of breathing. He admits not being any authority on yoga but feels that there is connection between yoga and vocal breath technique.

Back in Cornwall, Benjamin Luxon was recently performing in Camborne as part of the Kerrier Music and Dance Festival. In the programme he, with massed choirs, Camborne Town Band and the Bournemouth Symphonietta premiered "A Cornish Fantasia" by Cornish composer, Goff Richards. In July Benjamin will be conducting singing workshops for budding singers at the Newlyn Orion Gallery. He recognises the mass of natural music that is here in Cornwall and wants to nurture and expand it in whatever ways he can. Here then is a man at the height of his powers as a singer who wants to see the best in music for his native county. Right on.

Julia McLean

Sue Monro (June 1984)

The emergence of Theatre Rotto on the alternative Penwith cultural circuit has probably done more to liven up cabaret-style entertainment in the area than anything since the FestivalofFools. In fact it was Julia's involvement with the Barneys in the 1980 Festival of Fools that first brought her to Penwith ... "the area seemed so alive and full of possibilities on the theatrical side, I decided there and then to make it my home base." The group of performers and musicians she has gathered around her (collectively Theatre Rotto) now attract large, appreciative audiences both here and abroad.

From University to Agatha Christie

It must be one of life's strange little ironies that this dynamic, green-eyed, redhead with the perfect stage presence should have been born a clergyman's daughter. Her parents wanted her to have 'proper' job qualifications and she wanted to become an actress. In the end she compromised by doing a BA (Hons. Drama) at Manchester University; it proved to be time well spent, learning the basics of scriptwriting, producing, acting and testing out her own work in small studio groups. All the excitement and experimentation of university life evaporated when she joined the East 15 Acting School. Here the actor's ego had to be up front all the time, "We weren't encouraged to improvise or develop our own ideas, the emphasis was on stage technique and physical coordination." This was followed by a year teaching Drama and English at an East End school, then straight in at the deep end with a summer season playing support roles in Agatha Christie plays.

Stage Politics

In 1973 Julia joined the high-powered EMMA Theatre Co. which was set up to 'take theatre to the people' via the pub and club circuits, but it was here she made the break with conventional acting ... she wasn't impressed with their material. Most of the gags reinforced male stereotype attitudes towards women with all the usual crude jokes about female anatomy ... tits, melons and spaniel's ears...etc. (however Soiree evenings at the Union are redressing the balance!). It wasn't until she joined The Phantom Captain Fringe Co. that the chance came to improvise and work with the audience ... "It was a new approach then, based on the concept that it's better to put on material that is true to yourself, because then something real is likely to happen, we were reacting with people not stages." If anything, Phantom Captain was anti-theatre, based more on human failure than the usual ego-centric glamour image. This approach has been central to Julia's performances ever since. It has expanded and adapted over the years to encompass her own political conscience and growing state of awareness about the upheavals going on between men and women ... in fact for Julia sexual politics are the only politics, "Everything you look at has been created by the patriarchal society; the balance has to change radically before anything will change for the better; it is changing on a consciousness level but not in real terms." She would like to see many more women exerting their influence in positions of responsibility at the grass roots level, particularly in the entertainment world.

Phases and humour

Julia spent most of the '70s experimenting with different theatrical techniques and working through various phases before she felt confident enough to write and perform her own work on a professional basis ... "It was all part of my own maturing process both as an actress and as a person, the surreal element surfaced in 'Io,' her own metaphorical play which delved into the subconscious of a woman's relationship with inanimate objects. There was the bizarre, intensely personal 'Soubrettes'—a two-woman show about back-stage rivalries between two bunny girls. The tragic element came through in 'Ladybird'—the faded teenage idol whose life has been thwarted, she ends by making an impassioned plea to the women in the audience to be truer to themselves, to recognise their universal experiences in common, not to be passive and masochistic. Much of Julia's skill lies in her ability to externalise inner feelings in a way that other women can identify with; this is what makes her characters so powerfully real. Moreover she achieves this without resorting to the usual heavy sexist gags. Both male and female stereotypes are treated with equal irreverence ... take naughty Lola or Mr Wankitof for example. Making people laugh isn't always easy: "We have to change our act to suit the audience, you can't expect children, pensioners and trendy lefties to laugh at the same things." She doesn't set out to make any big statements but feels "it's good to do things which are just a bit on the line ... humour should be provocative rather than cathartic."

Theatre Rotto has provided Julla with a constantly adaptable melting pot into which she distills her own 20 years experience with the personalities, talents and ideas of her fellow performers ... " I like to look at a performer, see what they have to offer and put these things up front ... we've all grown together; it was mostly Tom's influence that brought out the comedienne in me. Of course, Tom is a natural actor with a very special style all of his own, he only has to munch an apple or mime antics to an old Roy Orbison song and everyone falls about laughing. Lucy has come a long way from complete novice; she has a real talent for transmitting enthusiasm to others; and Matthew, our most recent addition, has added his own magic, music and years of professional experience from Shiva Theatre." Julia has made a point of introducing new performers with fresh ideas to the cast, "otherwise we would be typecast as a little clique from Botallack."

Like most small theatre companies, Theatre Rotto is in desperate need of financial support. Considering they are the area's only live cabaret artists who continue to produce top quality entertainment for local people of all ages, a little help from SWA wouldn't be out of place!

Ken McMullen

Mike Venning (November 1986)

The centrepiece of this year's St Ives Autumn Film Festival was the showing of *Zina*, the latest film by British director Ken McMullen, who also came down to introduce the film and discuss it with the audience afterwards. This was quite a coup for the festival organisers as *Zina* is not yet on general release and has been picking up awards at international film festivals.

Zina is Ken McMullen's first 35mm feature film but he has been making films for some years. Much of his earlier work has been experimental and involved with performance art. He has collaborated with artist Stuart Brisley on several occasions, and his activity in this area reflects his earlier experience as a painter (he would still like to paint, but film-making leaves him too little time.

Ken's first two feature-length films were *Resistance* and *Ghost Dance*, both of which investigated the medium of film and ways of perception. He is interested in how we perceive and take in knowledge and experience, and one feels that the films are constructed in a similar fashion to the way that the brain receives and sorts information. *Ghost Dance*, for example, is in no way a straight narrative; images, characters and their words do not necessarily gel, there is no step-by-step sequence of events. The film is a multi-layered experience, whose fragments can be absorbed to form a coherent mosaic.

Concern with the underlying processes that are the foundations of our conscious perception is evident in *Ghost Dance*, which often undermines our expectations of film as a story with its flexible and fragmented characters, time and space. With *Zina* however, Ken McMullen seems to have gone for straight narrative. This film has a story and a definite set of constant characters. It is based on the last years of Zina, eldest child of Leon Trotsky, who, while her father was exiled to a Turkish island in the early 'thirties, was undergoing psycho-analysis in Berlin. Father and daughter, each in their own isolated way, see and prophesy the rise of fascism and its consequences. Trotsky is aware of the conscious, political movement of the times, while Zina feels the imminent threat, it invades her unconscious like a nightmare, finally becoming too great a burden and she commits suicide.

So, a narrative film, personal tragedy paralleled with the rising global catastrophe of the times. Yes and no: again: Ken looks way beneath the surface and weaves a net of the interconnecting events, experiences and psychological undertones that go to make up the supposedly logical sequences of history. Making psychoanalysis a central theme in the film colours everything else, particularly highlighting the way that Zina's mental aberrations become chilling reality for Europe in the decade after her death.

Ken McMullen's films are visually superb, shot after shot is beautifully composed and he intercuts colour sequences with black and white to great effect. *Zina* is also brilliantly paced, moving slowly and inexorably towards its tragic conclusion. He also writes his own scripts and does a great deal of his own research. In fact he is working on research for his next two projected films, one on Cromwell (fantastic, it's time someone got to grips with that great man), the other on the Paris Commune. A good director is also credited with the ability to bring out the best in his actors, and the performances by Ian McKellen, Domiziana Giordana and Philip Madoc in *Zina* are certainly excellent.

Using film in the way that Ken McMullen does opens up a vast range of possibilities. Cinema and television are young media utilised mainly for entertainment up to the present, but containing great power and scope for exploring areas still considered the realm of the written word or the static visual arts. *Zina* covers the microcosm of particular personal relationships, an array of the great events of the 20th century and the bottom line of human problems, the conflict between instinct and reason, left and right sides of the brain. It's enough to make a weighty tome but is all contained in a fascinating ninety minutes. Good for Goldstar Corporation for giving Penwith a preview of a film of this quality and the chance to pick its maker's brains. I hope they get Ken back when Cromwell's in the can.

Jacqui McShee

Martin Val Baker (February 1990)

Voice: You have been working with John, with Bert Jansch and also with the reformed Pentangle; can you tell us who's in the band at the moment?

JMcS: Well, there's me, Bert, Nigel Portman Smith plays fretless bass—though his main instrument is keyboards and we've just introduced them into the band, which is really nice—then there's Gerry Conway (of Fotheringay and Richard Thompson fame) on drums and Pete Kirtley on electric guitar. It's quite different from the early Pentangle stuff, though we do still do some of the early material because we still like it!

Voice: Who chooses the material? Does Bert still write?

JMcS: Bert still writes prolifically. I do some writing and Nigel does a bit. It's half and half contemporary and traditional. half and half new and old material.

Which do you prefer?

I like all of it! What we play is what we like to play We're actually all very polite; if we don t like something we just keep quiet and it becomes obvious and the idea is dropped But when people just get on with it and start playing we know that it's going to work

Is there any jazz in the set?

I'm trying to introduce more instrumentals but Bert keeps writing words for them. That really makes me cross!

If they do instrumentals, you can go to the bar.

No, I'm stuck on stage, but I can breathe deeply for a while!

Do you still work abroad a lot?

Yes, mainly America, Italy, Germany, Holland.

Do you enjoy the travelling?

To an extent, but it would be nice to work more In this country though things are changing slowly. I hate flying; I've had some nasty experiences lately.

You've been touring with Pentangle and also with John Renbourn and Tony Roberts, rushing around in different combinations. Don't you get confused?

Yes, sometimes I forget who I am, which repertoire.

Is the stuff you do with Bert vastly different from the stuff with John, are there any crossovers?

There's one crossover.

You must have a pretty large repertoire!

Yes, and if I work as a trio with Bert and Nigel, it's different again.

Would you like to do more solo numbers?

No, one unaccompanied number is enough in a set. You try to get as varied a set as possible to make it as interesting as possible for the people who are listening.

People ask for particular songs, is that a problem?

I find it strange. I was playing with John and someone asked for *Is It Real*, one of Bert's solos with the band. I shouldn't think John knows it and, working with Bert, someone asks for *Lord Franklyn*. No one else plays it like John.

Do you find songs or suggest them?

I don't put things forward unless I think they are going to be accepted—they're a pretty hard act to follow.

Have you ever wanted to be in complete control of an album—to pick your own songs and say, "I want Bert on that one, John on that one, the band on this one?"

I wouldn't mind doing one, picking the musicians I've had that worked out for quite some time. I've had several offers but they've always wanted to take control and not leave me any leeway at all and I've just said "No."

Would the record be mainly traditional or would you do new songs ?

A couple of years ago, when Mike Piggot played fiddle with Pentangle, we used to write songs together. That worked quite well.

He would do the music and you the words?

A bit of both.

Do you play an instrument?

Not in front of anybody; I pick out the tunes on a piano and then tape them.

Perhaps a small company could say "Right, Jacqui, go ahead, do the record?"

It's a nice thought—if it came up...

Maybe you could use Pentangle in variations. You could use John and Tony on one, Bert and Peter on another, Nigel on keyboards ... one of Danny Thompson's groups, with you as the common denominator.

There's lots of plans in my head.

Anything in the immediate future?

John and I hope to do a new album in the new year, mainly traditional. We haven't decided on the material yet, but we've had an offer and we're keen to do it.

Perhaps it could all take off again?

I just hope I've got the energy!

Albert Mellor "Cloggy"

Sue Monro (December 1983)

Stroll down Market Jew Street on Saturday morning and chances are you will come across one of Penzance's most cherished citizens. Uncle Albert or Cloggy (after the clogs he used to wear) with his barrel-organ, monkey and collection box has been a familiar sight to three generations of Cornish children for nearly half a century.

Albert was born in Rotterdam in 1890 where his father worked on the cargo barges. The family moved to England during the year of the great blizzard when Albert was just 3 months old. They lived as gypsies, travelling all over the country (including Ireland) selling their wares. Times were hard, particularly for a family trying to make a living out of traditional gypsy skills. Albert was forced to use every ounce of ingenuity just to stay alive ... it was either "work or starve". In fact he prospered, by the time he reached 10 he had saved £60 by selling camphor balls to householders. With this money in his pocket he set off by himself; it was to be the last contact he had with his family

He continued to peddle his way around the country, stopping over in favourite places from time to time. It wasn't until 1927 that he came to live in Cornwall which has been his 'home base' ever since, and it is here in West Penwith that he has become such a well-known figure. Farmers still question him about produce prices, crops and news of other areas ... he provides an excellent communication service (he never gossips!) ... not to mention a treat (usually chocolates or eggs) for the children that flock around his famous box.

As he talked about his experiences and described some of the people he had met and the countryside they lived in, I became aware of his outstanding visual memory, nothing seems to escape his attention, his descriptions were so vivid, it seemed as if he was talking about something that happened yesterday, not 50 years ago. But to recount all the many varied experiences he has had in the course of his long life one would need a lengthy book, (sadly this book is unlikely to be written, for Albert neither reads nor writes and has repeatedly turned down offers from other writers who have expressed interest in his life history). It would also offend his sense of natural dignity to have the details of his private life made public. It may seem curious that he has never had the urge to read or write, yet in the course of a brief conversation it became apparent he has survived remarkably well without the aid of books; for he possesses the kind of intuitive wisdom and has lead the sort of life that almost makes the written word redundant. At an early age he rebelled against society's conventional standards, replacing them with his own ways. It's given him a free hand to develop his own unique powers of perception, based on first-hand experience of life and people. Added to this, he has accumulated an intimate knowledge of the lore of the countryside ... everything from survival skills to the ways of animals, birds, plants and farmers. He knew where the birds laid their eggs, how to catch a rabbit, cook on an open fire and find shelter for the night. He remembers a Welsh farmer who was searching for some lost cows when he chanced along the same patch of road ... it was getting dark so Albert helped him find the cows and was duly offered a straw bed in the cowshed for the night, with the promise of a good breakfast if he mucked out the stables; he arose early and by the time the farmer appeared the whole place was spotless. The farmer complimented him on the fine job he had done and proceeded to moan about how difficult it was to find good workers ... it soon became obvious why no-one would work for him, for Albert was bade farewell without receiving his much anticipated breakfast. However the lady of the house took pity on him and came out with a cup of black tea and a slice of bread. There wasn't a trace of bitterness in his voice as he told this tale ... needless to say it didn't actually endear him to the Welsh— unlike the Crofters in Scotland who also had to struggle to survive but always managed to find him a slice of venison and a warm bed.

The Barrel Organs

It took Albert 20 years to save enough money to buy his barrel-organs. He purchased them from an Italian immigrant in Birmingham in 1919 (he has 2 of them, one over 100 years old) and despite numerous offers from collectors he has no intention of parting with them. He doesn't need much money to maintain his simple modest lifestyle "money's no value to me" ... his currency is based more on the fundamentals of trusting people, being cheerful, kind and helpful to others ... without any desire for recognition. He accepts people for what they are and judges them not on their worldly goods or position in society but rather on their spirit of generosity towards their fellow man. He commented "It's usually those who have the least to give who give the most". Over the years Albert has collected £40,000 for various charities which is no mean achievement.

Christmas is one of his busiest times of year, it always brings back memories of Christmases past when he, along with other travelling folk, took refuge in the workhouses, but rather than stay inside and join in the festive celebrations he took to the streets with his barrel-organ, to make his own, much preferring to be surrounded by a sea of happy smiling faces. For years he has given every baby born in the area around Christmas a silver ball to hang on the tree. Albert celebrates his 93rd birthday this month and his mind, memory and powers of observation are still as sharp as the early morning wind that blows in his face when he sets off with his organ and box of wares. His only regret is that his grandson doesn't share his enthusiasm for the barrel-organ, both for its earning capacity and the magic of being able to captivate an audience with its familiar tunes and timeless sounds. He commented that if he had his time all over again he wouldn't change a thing. I was lost in admiration for this gentle, happy man who has kept himself on the go and given so much pleasure, kindness and warmth to so many people.

John Michell

Mike Venning (October 1986)

John Michell began his interest in the old stones of Britain in the 'sixties out of a feeling of frustration at the arrogance of archaeologists. Why should it be that while it was obvious that no one really knew the whole story of megalithic culture, archaeologists wished to claim their theories as holy writ and reject all other suppositions? It's a strange paradox that science, which throughout history has considered itself to be pushing back the frontiers of knowledge, should be so dogmatic and blinkered. This illustrates the contradictory nature of the human psyche in that the discoveries of the inquisitive, exploratory side of the mind inevitably become dogmatized. Once static and drained of life however, the dogma is in turn swept away by a fresh wave of questioning and seeking.

Technology—
1. The terminology of a particular subject: technical language.

2. (a) The science of the application of knowledge to practical purposes: applied science.

(b) 1) The application of scientific knowledge to practical purposes in a particular field.

2) A technical method of achieving a practical purpose.

3. The totality of the means employed by a people to provide itself with the objects of material culture.

(*Webster's Third New International Dictionary*, 1961).

The contradiction that forms the base of human behaviour is an integral part of John Michell's view of history. He sees the megalithic remains as an artificial system, the technology of its time. Much of the meaning and power of the old stones was present in a more natural and therefore fragile or ephemeral state prior to the erection of the stones. However the development of culture created a need for the natural system to be recorded in a lasting manner. So stone, the most enduring material available, was used.

The cycle continues, because the definition of the stones produced dogma and with it a social class (eventually the Druids), self-appointed keepers of the privileged information that gradually enshrouded the meaning of the system. When, however, this caste became too arcane the wheel turned and they were discredited. Archaeologists (and all scientists) are examples of this same cyclic motion of systems. Theories only exist to be disproved and John is aware of this in his own field. He states that he does not hold to any grand theory which attempts to encompass all aspects of stone-age culture. He talks in an almost throwaway style, easy come, easy order here, his theories are there to be blown just like all the rest.

He has taken more interest in the practical and concrete aspects of the remains of megalithic culture. He doesn't give the impression that he is expecting to find the meaning of life half-hidden in the bracken around Boscawen-un circle. In fact, rather than treating the whole thing as a prehistoric ivory tower to be scaled only by the aware elite, he seems to incline towards a view of prehistory as a part of the shifting, convoluted development of humanity, not always as far away and mysterious as it is often made out to be. Perhaps the stones should be enjoyed for what they now are, beautiful and fascinating remains of the unreclaimable past, fuel for the imagination but not fodder for fantasy The sheer lack of knowledge about these artefacts has made them objects of interest throughout history. The speculation ranges from localised folk history to the lunatic fringe of extrapolation theories.

Running steadily and centrally through all this is a tradition of antiquarian study, from Aubrey and Stukeley through such Cornish examples as Borlase and Blight to the present and John Michell himself. Dr. Stukeley used to take parties of friends to Avebury or Stonehenge and entertained the aristocracy with his views on the Druids as well as producing a body of serious studies of the ancient sites. John's presence in Penzance last month was to guide a party of visiting Americans around the stone relics of Penwith, and to do so in a civilised but pleasurable manner; not rubbernecking and ain't it cuteness, but genuine interest in and enjoyment of the distant past.

In connection with this antiquarian viewpoint locally, John Michell has written a book on J.T. Blight, a native of Penzance, whose drawings, engravings and research into the antiquities of this area in the last century have not been equalled. Sadly Blight ended his life in the madhouse; somehow one doesn't feel that the same fate awaits John. He has spent a long time studying the old stones, conclusions have been reached; some, one feels, have been rejected later, but out of it all has come a great love for the stone system and the ancient sites. John Michell can and does take pleasure in these old places and perhaps that's a more important aspect than many would have us believe.

John Miller

Sue Monro (April 1984)

Painting the landscape, is for John Miller, a way of celebrating life. "We have to be still and silent if we are to know the land, we need to know the land before we can paint it, we must not only look at it, we must listen to it and smell it ... we have to enter into it like explorers. He feels the camera can capture the image and atmosphere of a place but the artist must penetrate through that image to possess and be possessed by the force of life itself .

John spent most of his early life in London and only took up professional painting after pursuing a variety of occupations. These years are perhaps best described by his lifelong friend, the writer John le Carré†.. ('The stage had him, and lost him ... he would have made an excellent actor... A successful architectural practice ended abruptly, one may now say providentially, with an unpleasant accident to his drawing hand. Intermittently he turned his penetrating eye upon the antiques business and I like to believe that to this day, he holds some sort of record for selling the best things with the least profit. This was a period when his relationship with life was so exuberant that he felt it unreasonable that he should be paid for anything that gave him satisfaction. Alas, he was applying the tender standards of a creative artist to a trade not celebrated for its tenderness")

John first came to Cornwall in 1958, as an architectural student to measure the screen at St. Buryan Church, but it was the landscape that captured his imagination ... so much so that he immediately resolved to make Cornwall his adopted home. He used his architectural training to earn a living and undertook a wide range of commissions ... everything from stage and interior design to plans for cottage conversions, but painting soon came to occupy more and more of his time and the turning point in his career came in 1974 when John Halkes encouraged him to exhibit at the Newlyn Orion. It was a huge success and his paintings have been in constant demand from Galleries and private collectors ever since.

This fine Georgian house, set in spacious, rambling gardens and crammed with fascinating objects has been John's home since 1964 ... It's not only the resident colony of rooks that have found sanctuary in this peaceful centre of Sancreed. Over the years John has established, with the help of Michael Truscott (himself a distinguished potter and internationally recognised picture framer) both a spiritual base and working co-operative for many young artists and craftsmen. John described it as a loose-knit, harmonious community that has grown organically to suit the needs and aspirations of everyone there at any given time. Scores of people have benefitted from its therapeutic atmosphere ... some arrived with problems and needed a quiet space to rebuild their lives and others were attracted by the stimulating, creative environment. A pottery and chalets were built in the gardens to cater for their needs. Sadly the pottery had to be closed for economic reasons and Michael now concentrates mainly on restoration work. The print and framing business has flourished, it keeps 2 skilled craftsmen fully occupied. Their vast selection of top quality frames are amongst the finest in this country. Much hard work and organization goes into keeping the centre running smoothly, yet in spite of the constant hum of industrious activity a sense of calm and joy comes from everyone there. It came as no surprise to discover that this generosity of spirit is very much part of the Franciscan tradition, three of the team are lay monks/companions of the Order of St. Francis. The care and concern they show towards each other is extended to all who have soug ht refuge with them, (the same gentle eye John casts over his landscapes is also extended towards humanity")

For a long time John saw the painter's world as an exclusive club to which he lacked the vital entry ticket, it wasn't until he stopped trying to be a painter and just walked into the landscape and painted it, that he discovered his own personal vision and sense of direction. He is the first to admit that much about painting is sheer hard work; he constantly puts his talents to the test through an arduous process of discovery and elimination. Yet the joy he feels from the creative process of totally absorbing himself in a landscape makes every minute worthwhile. One can well imagine he would still be painting with the same dedication even if he had never sold a single painting ... this is not to say he is unconcerned about other people's reactions "a painter wants to communicate, if nobody wants to share it with you, then you are failing." He doesn't see himself as a great painter, for him the only gift is vision, but he is pleased to receive letters from people who have purchased a painting and through it discovered a new way of looking at a landscape, "if occasionally, people get something from your work, you can ask for nothing more."

The paintings of Turner are frequently mentioned when people try to describe John's work: it's true they share the same intense feeling for light along with a timeless, mystical quality that draws the eyes across vapourized spaces into a distant world just beyond our vision, but where Turner included human figures and mythological themes in his work, John prefers to concentrate on the sheer power of the scenery "the problem with 'peopling' a landscape is that the landscape has a quality which you want to enter into ... if the people are there already, then perhaps you are not drawn into it so readily". He does make the occasional exception, as in his remarkable series of paintings that illustrate the history of St. Michael's Mount.

He finds the scale of commission work quite a challenge, and this particular series gave him a great deal of satisfaction, not least because of the understanding and generous encouragement shown to him by Lord and Lady St. Levan. In 1980 he completed a superb allegorical painting showing an aerial view of Cornwall, with a procession of Cornish saints hovering above the spires of Truro Cathedral. Again, it was his vibrant rendition of light that caught the imagination ... the symbolism of the setting sun as its fading rays are replaced by the radiance of Christianity, with the firmament of earth and sky linked by a thread of light. But the Cornwall he most frequently paints is the land of mists and mellow patchwork pastures, storm clouds gathering over Sancreed, a church tower isolated by a patch of light or windswept trees silhouetted against a distant horizon.

John approaches his landscapes with the reverence and application of a scientist, mystic or explorer. That they positively radiate joy, light and colour and are so universally understood is no small measure of their success.

† With thanks to John le Carré for quotes taken from Messum Gallery Exhibition Catalogue.

Denis Mitchell

Sue Monro (November 1985)

"God has given me the ability to be an artist, there is nothing in using this gift, only to be utterly ashamed if I do not"

Denis isn't sure who to credit with this quote but he feels it so aptly sums up his own creative life that it could have been written with him in mind. He admits it took a long time and many diversions before he fully recognised his potential as a sculptor and even then circumstances played a significant role ... being in the right place at the right time, surrounded by friends, family and other artists who gave him encouragement, support and stimulation. Yet in his unassuming way (he insists he is just getting on with what he has to do) this prolific carver of wood/stone/metal, has, over 30 years, produced some exceedingly fine work which in terms of purity of form and finish must surely rank alongside the work of his former 'teacher' Barbara Hepworth.

Denis was 18 when he first came from Swansea to live in Cornwall in 1930. An aunt had purchased a derelict cottage near St. Ives; together with his brother Endell, they renovated it and stayed on to make a living out of market-gardening. St. Ives was already well-established as an artists' colony. Denis found himself intoxicated with "all its romance of artists and their studios, the smell of linseed oil and turps was inspiration in itself"

Only later he came to realise "that with the exception of a few, most painters were not very good", but that also worked in reverse ... he remembers seeing "a bent old fisherman sitting outside his house with paintings arranged on orange boxes." At the time, he considered them 'childish' but now cherishes the Alfred Wallis paintings hanging on his wall.

During this period he started to paint representational landscapes, but with characteristic humility considered them too unprofessional to exhibit, so the task of earning a living occupied most of his time and energy. Fortunately he was good with his hands and willingly adapted his practical skills to everything from ploughing fields to carpentry. Frequently jobs brought him into contact with other artists. It was his Home Guard companion, Bernard Leach, who recommended him to Barbara Hepworth who needed an assistant for 3 days whilst she was preparing for an exhibition. Little did he realise he would stay for 11 years, become her chief assistant and in later years an extension of her right hand.

Apart from a few woodcarvings, Denis had never done any serious sculpture before working for Barbara. He readily acknowledges his debt to her ... "to have worked and been friends with two such professional artists as Barbara and Ben Nicholson was an education in itself ... she had a fantastic eye for form, time was no object to her, unless she was absolutely satisfied with the final shape ... even on a very large carving, less than a hair's breadth rubbed off could alter the whole sculpture."

Under her exacting eye he acquired the rare capacity to work and concentrate on his own. sculpture for 8 hours a day. In retrospect, he sees some disadvantages in working under such a powerful influence; so many of his creative years went into Barbara's work and many more years were to elapse before he established a style that was totally his own.

Looking around his studio in Newlyn it is difficult to believe that such a diversity of shapes and finishes could all have come from the same hands and yet they all display a feeling of unity and wholeness that makes them part of the same family. Perhaps this comes from his method of working, each piece starts the same way...meticulously worked out on the sketchpad (he is loathe to intellectualise about his sources of inspiration, they all flow from his experience of life) and then, for metal sculptures, he builds up a rough form in plaster which is sand cast into a block, he then painstakingly sets about coaxing it into the desired shape. Each piece has a myriad of contrasting qualities ... spiky bronze corkscrews with silky smooth surfaces ... serene, undulating forms vibrant with female energy ... all abstract but full of humanity. He likes to keep his work around him for a long time, constantly refining and thinking about it. All his work has an enduring, lovingly crafted feeling which may explain why they are so highly prized by their new owners. He will only sell to people who genuinely like a sculpture for itself, not for its investment value. He has exhibited all over the world and has made a point of naming his work after Cornish villages . . . he found when he put a name on a sculpture the public would spend hours trying to relate the work to the title and miss out on all its other qualities, a perfect example of this occurred when he was exhibiting with the British Council in Indonesia...an enthusiastic critic commented "this is a most interesting exhibition, you have to look very carefully, for every piece is derived from cats," it seems the works were listed in the catalogue as Cat. 1, Cat. 2 etc!

One of the greatest lessons Barbara Hepworth inadvertently taught Denis (he considered the loneliness, isolation and lack of humour in her life resulted from her .obsessional dedication to sculpture) is that Art is not the only thing in life. Family life, human relationships and a wide spectrum of other interests and activities, whether it was working underground at Geevor and sharing innermost thoughts with fellow miners or pub-crawling with Dylan Thomas, have all provided invaluable feedback that goes directly into his sculpture and bounces back as pure energy.

An exhibition of his work, including a selection of his working drawings, will be on show at the Newlyn Orion from 1st-27th November.

Paul Mount

Sue Monro (March 1984)

Henry Moore once said "because a piece of sculpture does not aim at reproducing natural appearances it is not, therefore an escape from life but more an expression of the significance of life". This is particularly true of Paul Mount's sculpture. Most of his designs are abstract, occasionally inspired by the human form or the shapes of the natural world ... wings poised for flight, an opening flower or a weathered boulder, but, essentially, his work exhibits a deep affinity with the energies of life rather than an emulation of its forms.

Paul was born in 1922 at Newton Abbot. He was determined from childhood to become a painter and was encouraged in this by sympathetic parents who both taught at the grammar school where he was educated. His Art School training was conventional ... 3 years general art studies at a provincial art school during which time he learned the basics of modelling and casting, followed by 3 years at the Royal College of Art in London. After the war he taught painting at Winchester School of Art and then in 1955 went out to Nigeria to run an Art Department at Yaba College. It was during this period he started to work with three dimensional forms, initially inspired by the wood carving done by the West Africans and later through the encouragement of two architects Borys and Atkinson who commissioned him to design eight architectural sculptures. In 1962 Paul returned to Cornwall and set up a studio in St. Just where he still lives with his wife June Miles, the painter. At first there was little demand for architectural sculpture so he turned to smaller pieces, but it wasn't long before the urge to do larger works returned and he started to experiment with stainless steel. The local blacksmith Jim Williams taught him how to weld, he attended classes in finishing techniques and was fortunate in having the co-operation of the staff at the Neale Talbot Foundry at Hayle. He returns to smaller works from time to time and even does the occasional painting but it is the larger works he tackles with most enthusiasm, Architectural Sculpture.

It is in this field that Paul has established his reputation as a skilled, inventive designer, it is also the area in which he finds some of the most rewarding challenges ... the exploration of new materials, balancing out the functional purpose of a building with the artistic nature of a sculpture and the co-operation required to produce a good working partnership with the architect. Ideally this collaboration should start when the building is still on the drawing board ... this makes it possible to consider the proportions of the building in relation to the size and style of the sculpture required. He frequently works with local. architect John Crowther who allows him a sufficient degree of flexibility in interpretation which enables him to explore more freely the world of pure form. Most of his constructions are made of fibreglass, concrete or steel; he passes on the designs in the form of engineering drawings, models or templates to contractors who carry out the work. He has recently completed a large stainless steel mobile for a shopping centre in Harlow. It is powered by an electric motor which makes it revolve on pivots ... from these points stress and balance interact with the drama of intersecting swords of steel which cut diagonals through the air ... multiple perspectives open and replace each other, shimmering, polished surfaces catch and play with the light ... the total effect is breathtaking. He manages to combine the precision and skill of an inventor with the fertile imagination of an artist.

Nothing gives more distinction to Paul's work than his inherent understanding and feeling for different materials, and his recognition that a theme that could be explored in one material would lose its meaning all together in another. The unyielding nature of iron is used to heighten the image of a dictator ... stubborn, jagged block rhythms blend with hard angular lines, wood is more supple and lends itself to soft undulating curves that echo the human body, the tension of stainless steel is reflected in his mobiles which take exhilarating risks as they alter direction, break, rear and capture the very principles of motion. He welds the abstract principles of sculpture with the realisation of an idea by giving outward form to inner feelings through the manipulation of solid materials. Full appreciation of his work demands an effort from the observer, it arouses our curiosity and sharpens our senses. Our imaginations are seduced into exploring vacant spaces, we are encouraged to view the whole work from within, to follow the subtle transition of one shape merging into another and learn how to appreciate the shape simply as a shape, not as a description or representation of something else. His work encourages self-discovery, this stops it from remaining outside the desires and necessities of everyday life.

Paul's work is represented in collections throughout Europe, America and Nigeria. He holds regular exhibitions in London at the New Arts Centre and has a permanent collection on display at his home/studio at Nancherrow, St. Just. He has completed 24 large scale architectural sculptures for public and commercial buildings, including a splendid multi-dimensional frieze for the Co-op at Camborne. He must surely rate as one of the area's most imaginative artists who uses his talent to enhance the environment.

PTURE AT
twentieth century sculpture
Wells Cathedral to celebrate
H ARMITAGE
L AYRTON
HADWICK
TH FRINK
BARB
JOHN
DENIS
PAUL
dral cloister, Wells, Som
October 1982 Open da

Jo O'Cleirigh

Sue Monro (November 1983)

"Whatever advances we feel we have made beyond our 'primitive' fore-bears, in many ways we still share the same needs and emotions as they did. With all our increased knowledge of the world, life itself seems if anything more mysterious now than it probably did then. The little circle of light representing knowledge has grown apace, yet by virtue of its expansion it has increased its points of contact with the unknown, and the mystery deepens".

Jo O'Cleirigh has spent most of his life seeking, exploring and experiencing points of contact with the unknown. It has taken him on archaeological expeditions to discover more about the ways of our ancestors, it has lead him on a spiritual quest through Catholicism, the Jesuit Order and finally to Neopaganism.

Jo remembers the awe and wonderment of the childhood days he spent exploring the ancient shrines and wells in the Lostwithiel area ... he remembers visiting the Plymouth City Museum to investigate the origins of an old oil lamp. It was here a whole new world of learning and knowledge opened up to him, it awakened in him a fascination with the esoteric and the search began to trace and connect the roots, mysteries and culture of past civilisations with the social and spiritual states of present day society.

He left school at 15 without formal training in any trade and took on various manual jobs until National Service training dispatched him to the Canal Zone in Egypt. On returning to Plymouth he took a bus driving job and volunteered his spare time to the City Museum and spent weekends on digs. In 1965 he started his first full-time job in Archaeology as assistant in the Inspectorate of Ancient Monuments. The work involved excavation of 3 huge late Neolithic monuments in Wiltshire. As his knowledge and experience grew he applied for more ambitious projects ... from 1965 onwards he has taken part in 19 major expeditions to Egypt and two on the site of Kommos in Crete. One of the most challenging proved to be the Akhenaten Temple project where 45,000 photographs of inscribed blocks were studied and pieced together. More recently his attention has centred on the artistic side of archaeological draughtsmanship ... doing working drawings to illustrate books and last year he painted a 9ft. square replica of the Shrine of Osiris in the Canadian Institute in Cairo.

Most of the digs were on sacred ceremonial sites ... he recalls reading Robert Graves' book The White Goddess and being suffused with the whole atmosphere of Goddess worship as well as being fascinated by the symbolism and social climate of pre-Christian religion. But the seeds of his own search were sown many years earlier ... as a child he was enchanted by the sensual aspects of Catholicism ... its sights, sounds, music, incense etc. and for many years he was a devout Catholic. In the mid-50s he spent a year with the Jesuits studying for the priesthood. But orthodox religion left many of his questions unanswered: the dogma and closed world of a hierarchical order where theology was more important than his own direct numinous experiences proved too restrictive. He saw their concepts of sin, guilt and divine retribution as sad misunderstandings of normal growth experiences. He felt that people were meant to live lives filled with joy, love, pleasure and humour. He came to recognise over a long period through constant inner questioning (to the extent of tracing the roots of Catholicism back some 35,000 years to pagan times) that Neopagan philosophy had much in common with his own.

One of Jo's most pressing concerns is the way in which the natural environment and ecology of the planet is being abused and destroyed by what he described as "3,000 years of the patriarchy with its Abrahamic concept of man's separation from nature" ... "The myths and symbols which underlie and still guide our secular society are those of the monotheistic religions which denigrate nature and woman and perpetuate those "male" values and traits of dominance and aggression." It is for this reason he lays so much stress on the Goddess presence in deity and feminine values ... intuitive, receptive, nurturing, loving and concerned with relationships with all parts of life. The rape of the Earth, the alienation of people from the rest of the cosmos goes together with, and is partly caused by, the suppression of the 'female' in our lives. He is also concerned about the plight of the native peoples of the Earth whose sacred tribal lands, cultural heritage and whole way of life is threatened by western industrial patterns. He, along with all Neopagans, actively support the Green Movement, CND, FOE and the Onaway Trust, (set up to assist native peoples) ... "We are in a symbiotic relationship with the Earth and what we do to its physical and spiritual resources is what we are doing to ourselves."

To a certain extent Neopagans are modern day heirs to the ancient mystery traditions as well as to the more popular festivals and seasonal rites. They make no distinction between spiritual and material, sacred and secular, there are no contradictions between their concern for political and social change and their concern for 'things of the spirit' which they equate with the need for beauty or that spark that creates a poem or a dance. Jo feels one of Neopaganism's most refreshing aspects is the absence of missionary zeal that other religions use to attract converts. For him it was simply an extension and reaffirmation of previously-held convictions and experiences. There are no formal rigid structures or authoritarian rulers, only small loose-knit groups of individuals who come together to celebrate an aspect of their shared beliefs. Their polytheistic world view allows a wider range of choices, the individual can identify with different deities at different times. They are wary of monotheism with its constant calls for unity and integration ... "it has been misappropriated throughout history when small groups of people wanted to control large numbers of people." Perhaps the polytheistic affirmation of diversity has come at a time when many people increasingly fear complexity, and accept authoritarian solutions.

Jo hopes to assist in the setting up of a Centre in Penwith. Its aims will be to create in people a basic consciousness of the sacredness of life ... "somehow we have to reclaim the Earth from those who have lost their respect and reverence for her. To bring together the insights of ecology, womanspirit and native wisdom such as that of the American Indians with our own Pagan inheritance. It will be dedicated to rebuilding Culture ... anything less is not enough."

Anyone interested in helping to start the Centre of Gaia please write to: Jo O'Cleirigh (Clarke), Chy-an-Goverrow, Lamorna, Penzance.

The following books are recommended by Jo to anyone interested in following up some of the points raised in this article:

The Death of Nature ... Carolyn Merchant

Woman and Nature ... Susan Griffen

Reclaim the Earth. Anthology from Women for Life on Earth

Basic Call to Consciousness ... M. Indian

Drawing Down the Moon ... Margot Adler

The Spiral Dance ... Starhawk.

Jane O'Malley

Jody Stewart (May 1988)

The light was a thin grey-blue as though, beneath the hazy sky, sea spray had filtered through the enormous window stretching its eye from Clodgy to the Island across Porthmeor Beach. The chill air made a sting in the nose, that studio smell, the room itself held an ordered disarray where only the artist's sure instinct and sense of habitation allowed her to alight on just that picture or object she required (though work is only numbered and catalogued as it leaves the studio).

Each morning, Jane O'Malley opens the curtains in the cottage she shares with her husband, the painter Tony O'Malley, to read the weather. In St Ives, windows 'keep you from being hemmed in.' The windows in her home, and the studio window often frame her paintings, for Jane O'Malley chooses to concern herself with still life. It's often the accident of what just happens to be there at the moment that starts her drawing either on pads or in her 'visual diaries', bound books she can carry anywhere which record the instants of her days and the objects which fill them.

"I love the simplicity of one shape" she declares with the sort of homage most of us would like to feel toward what surrounds us, but "I would never set up a still life." She would only delete an object which didn't interest her, or vary the colours. The 'diaries', with their accumulated hundreds, perhaps thousands, of drawings, capture vases, pots and flowers but only the occasional landscape or person. Jane can recall the events of a day, even its dramas, just by glancing at what she'd drawn.

Jane O'Malley was born and raised in Beloeil, Canada, a town just outside Montreal beside the Richelieu River. The river mattered, and she has always needed to be near water. When young she spent a good deal of time drawing flowers, sometimes through a magnifying glass. Perhaps it was then she became fascinated with line and shape, the lines suggesting what a shape might contain. Since her father was English, she travelled to London in 1963, at the age of nineteen, to visit relatives. She took a secretarial job and was too busy and distracted to draw. Later she travelled with her brother as far as Australia and Japan, but when she was scheduled to return home she couldn't bear to set foot on the boat. To earn money, and with hopes of improving her French, she worked abroad as an au pair and started drawing again "the barns and corners" of Switzerland.

When the job finished, she began looking for an art school which would avoid the academic crunch and found her way to St Ives in September 1969 to study at Leonard Fuller's St Ives School of Painting.

September, and the sea caused her to fall in love with the town, but before long loneliness had her planning to go back to Canada after nearly seven years away. That January she met Tony O'Malley, and only briefly returned home to make some money. She came to stay in 1971, and went to work full-time on her art. Since then she and Tony have been able to spend thirteen winters in the Bahamas where slowly another sort of painting became activated for Jane by immersion in that soft, lush world, which contrasted so absolutely with St Ives. This experience, which often entailed painting outdoors, evolved to make larger, wilder, airy—but not ethereal—paintings, a number of which will be shown at the Penwith Gallery this June.

Jane and Tony continue to travel, spending time on the Scillies and part of each summer in Ireland. As Jane says, "St Ives is an inward place. I think you have to get out of it."

She is fortunate to have the continual counterpoint of varied landscapes, light, and interiors to both balance and constantly wrench her into freshening perceptions. It was on the Scillies with only one table in their cottage, that Jane and Tony found they could easily share the same work surface and both get on with it unselfconsciously.

Jane feels she must try to work every day and chooses to organise herself so that is possible. In the summer she may get up very, very early, go a few doors down to the studio, and feel she has done 'a day's work' by 8am. In the autumn she's drawn to her window in late afternoon; she particularly loves the light as it quickly darkens. There are several recent paintings of anemones against a crepuscular window; the heavy dusk pressing toward the flowers like the water itself while the flowers deepen their colours (even more than anemones already do) against it as though they were torches holding off the night. These paintings show an immediate brush work which is a diversion from Jane's usual technique. She may use oil on hardboard, or the quicker softer oil on paper which blurs at the edges so that it is shape, not line, which we attend to—shape almost chewed at the edges. But most often, working from a drawing, Jane uses a knife to build up a line which the rest of the painting forms around.

"Drawing with a knife creates something absolutely precise which you are then stuck with."

Then, slowly, she spreads layers of glaze so that many colours eventually show through each other. So while the vase, flower, or whatever are merged with their background and feel organically related to it, these subjects also just barely seem to float on the surface of the ground. The effect is that your eye feels it has singled out the object all by itself, has chosen it, feeling intimate and tenderly toward it.

Jane also works with gouache on paper, acrylic, and has at least one pad filled with remarkable drawings in conte crayon which have a special modulated sensuousness and are spectacular in themselves.

Jane O'Malley's still life exhibition at The Salt House Gallery, St Ives (her twelfth one-person show) will be on throughout April. From her more stylised 'studio' (her word) paintings to her looser, more immediate work, there will be plenty to look at and perhaps we, like the painter, will become addicted to certain objects and visions of objects. Perhaps we may re-see them as she does each time she sits down to draw, or paint a favourite thing which just happens to be there by a window where so much of seeing itself happens.

Tony O'Malley

Mike Venning (October 1986)

Tony O'Malley's studio is filled with paintings of all shapes and sizes, canvasses and wooden constructions crowd the walls, vibrant colour shines out everywhere. Thus it is with his life; Tony is immersed in painting; it's a daily occurrence, as natural as eating or cleaning his teeth. The paintings owe their existence to Tony, and conversely, he finds himself in his paintings.

There are no limits, barriers or dogmas in Tony O'Malley. He keeps a visual diary, paints and draws from life, makes constructions and works constantly on a stream of studio paintings. To him this is all one process, a drawing may trigger off an idea for a studio picture, images from one piece of work get reworked as a part of another, but there is no differentiation. He doesn't like the word 'art', it defines and confines too much. What he does is his means of expressing himself; it happens to involve using paint, canvas, pencils or crayons, and he just gets on with it.

Getting on, doing, these are operative words to Tony. Thinking about painting, poetry or music is fine but nothing gets done unless you get on with the job. Thinking can turn into a philosophy of art which is too claustrophobic for him. It can also bypass the creative process by reaching conclusions that preclude any need for practical work. All this sort of definition removes the mystery from painting and that's where the magic lies for him.

The Irish love of words and the sheer music of language has been transposed in Tony to a love of colour, marks and images. This appears in every picture as colours cascade, sometimes in waves and veils of gestural marks, or maybe in strong but subtle shades. The language of painting entrances him and is demonstrated by his constructions. These enter his life as pieces of driftwood that catch his eye while out walking but once in his hands they are destined to be fitted together and transformed with colour into extensions of himself. Words and language are too precise for Tony. That precision cuts out the nuances and echoes that he wishes to include in what he expresses. His painting cannot simply be categorised, figures materialise in seemingly abstract pictures, landscape appears non-representational.

There's nothing mystical about Tony O'Malley. He would probably be more in tune with Hamlet—'There are more things in heaven and earth, Horatio, than are contained within your philosophy.' He is open to all possibilities, a receptive eye responding to stimuli from outside and within. He is sensitive to environment. He likes places where life is going on or evidence of man's past activities is still visible. When drawing up at Ding Dong he feels the presence of the old miners and the whole community that was there in the past while taking in the landscape as it is now. Every summer he returns to his home town in Ireland and autumn usually sees him in the Isles of Scilly. These places have their particular effect on his work yet all are fairly similar. Recently his winters have been spent in the Bahamas which has proved quite a contrast to his usual haunts, and it certainly shows in the paintings. He is showing pictures from the Bahamas at the Newlyn Orion Gallery at present and their sparkling, sun-lit tropical colours do differ markedly from the temperate hues of the work done in Ireland and Cornwall.

While not wishing to make Tony seem parochial, for his work is universal like all good painting, his celtic heritage is important. His vision is an organic synthesis in which the material world merges naturally with the atmosphere of the past and a flow of images from the unconscious. Even listening to him talk is a liberating experience as he moves beyond the constrictions of the English language. He is bilingual and doesn't have to confine himself to thinking in English. His paintings have the same natural freedom and are relaxed and flowing while never becoming casual. And himself—he's letting what's natural to him happen, while the rest of us should be happy to have Tony O'Malley here in Penwith.

George Ordish

Mercia Kemp (March 1986)

He had warned me, "Visitors are known to get lost and die of hunger while trying to find my home." But the weather was with me as I set forth on the only brilliantly sunny day of February and, after much roaming in muddy lanes, reading of maps and consultations with friendly farmers, I arrived at George Ordish's garden.

In his book, *The Living Garden* he writes "The word 'garden' comes from the Hebrew and means 'a pleasant place', and it is to this Eden that each. gardener, after his or her fashion, strives to return." George returned to his little Eden in Nancledra after many years of travelling the world. His life has been and is a very full one. He worked as economic entomologist for the United Nations, the FAO and the Ministry of Overseas Development. He has written many books about insects, his life-long love, about South American cultures and, with Pearl Bailey, a fascinating novel *Ladies Only* on feminism, multinational interests and chemical warfare which, in the early 'sixties, was making points that we ordinary people are only now, in the mid-'eighties, beginning to discern.

And yet, while I stand in awe at his accomplishments, he manages to make it all sound as a succession of coincidences. "Tell me about the beginning of your interest in insects"—"Oh, I don't know, I think it was the entomology teacher at London University, I liked him, he drank a lot, and I saw him at the pub. He made very good slides but we rarely got to see them. His hands trembled so much that he couldn't get them in the slot.".

"Tell me about your success with books"—"Well, that is all down to my agent, Deborah Owen, she's very good." His books have been published in many languages. He shows me the Japanese translation of one of his books about butterflies.

"Authors are supposed to proofread and approve the translated manuscript, you know," he says, with an impish grin.

Here in Nancledra we sit, drinking coffee, the sun miraculously pouring through the window, and George Ordish takes me for a guided tour of his memories.

"I was in Cuba just before the revolution. Batista was a rogue. And Castro, he wasn't a dyed in the wool Communist, you know, he tried to get help from the Americans but they wouldn't grant it, so it had to be Russia. I was in Nicaragua many times, I remember arriving at the tiny airport in Managua once, and a friend of mine whisking me to a party at the presidential palace. I had no suitable clothes so I had to wear my friend's father-in-law's second best suit. The palace was magnificent. It seemed that Somoza had spent a lot of the nation's wealth in decorating it, in true dictator's fashion. They didn't have a hospital, but their president had a magnificent home.".

I asked him to tell me what he feels about the present situation in Nicaragua; "Oh, Reagan is obsessed with Communism. He is a third rate brain and lazy at that. I read something in the *New Yorker* the other day which I think highlights the way many Americans think. It said 'How is the President so afraid of a country with a population the size of Brooklyn?'"

More anecdotes follow. We travel the Americas and Africa and arrive in Spain. "I was in Seville shortly after the war. With some friends, I wanted to travel by car to Barcelona on the coastal roads. We were told there was no petrol to be had. Our driver tried the blackmarket with no success so eventually I went to see a friend of mine who owned the match factory. He let us have the petrol from their fire engine. I don't know what would have happened if there had been a fire that night! But I was able to tell the driver, 'You need a foreigner to get you petrol!'" That grin again.

I ask him about his work.

"Yes, we knew that DDT would have to be phased out. It didn't work after a few years, because the insects became immune to it, but also, it wasn't just the conservationists that were against it, you see. The big companies were against it because it was too cheap and anyone could make it. There was no money to be made in DDT.".

"I think, on the whole, international organisations, specially the FAO, are doing good work. They have exceptional difficulties because of political interference. The anti-locust organisation, for instance. To deal with locusts is fairly easy provided you do it at a time when there are no locusts but this is expensive and also you get difficulties with neighbouring countries not allowing you to cross their frontiers and so on. There are often political considerations which stop the work being done.".

We move on to the present. His very successful books, *The Living House* and *The Living* Garden are being re-printed. *The Living House* is the history, spanning four hundred years, of the inter-action of living things in a farmhouse in Kent. Eighteen generations of humans and up to four thousand generations of non-humans populate its pages. *The Living* Garden follows the same plot in the garden of the house. *The Economist* described *The Living House* as 'A book about men, women and children, mice, weevils, dogs, lice, bats, house-martins, domestic architecture, social history and evolution.' Absolutely not to be missed, if you haven't read them yet.

His new project is a fascinating one. He's researching the life of Dona Marina, a young Mexican Indian woman of great intelligence, who was Hernan Cortez's interpreter and secretary. "He could not have conquered Mexico without her," he says, "not only did she interpret for him, but she gave him political counsel."

A colleague of his is researching the lives of two other women who also helped change the future of Latin America but whom history has chosen to forget. A Brazilian princess, daughter of King Pedro II, who, during a short period of regency, abolished slavery in Brazil, in the early nineteenth century, and an Englishwoman who married a Paraguayan dictator. The three stories will eventually be published in one volume.

"Don't you miss your travels now, George?"

"Oh no, I've done travelling. A friend of mine, a great traveller, was telling me the other day that he was 'doing' the wall of China this year. I replied that this year I was doing Carbis Bay.".

In his private Eden in Nancledra, with the lake teaming with the insects that he loves and the house full of images and words, and memories, sits George Ordish. But he's not resting.

George Ordish's *The Living House* and *The Living Garden* are both published by Bodley Head.

Clive Palmer

Martin Val Baker (May 1984)

One of the notable phenomena of the nineteen-sixties and -seventies was the increasing popularity of a broad-based 'Folk' music throughout the country. Starting with a revival of the Folk tradition, the genre moved on to a highly-creative phase which helped revolutionise British popular music. One of the most influential groups of this period was the INCREDIBLE STRING BAND, whose records of the late 'sixties set a marker for others to follow. (Both John Lennon and Bob Dylan admitted to a liking for the ISB.) Playing on the first String Band LP was Banjoist and multi-instrumentalist Clive Palmer, now, 18 years on, working as a woodwork teacher in West Cornwall.

Clive Palmer was born in London in 1943 and took an early interest in the banjo, receiving lessons in the classical style from virtuoso Alfred Lloyd, a former partner of the legendary banjoist Joe Morley. In 1961 Clive met guitarist WIZ JONES and began to play in the Folk style at various London clubs in the company of such as John Baldry, Rod Stewart and Davey Graham, eventually spending two years with Wizz in France.

In 1963 Clive moved to Scotland where another hive of creativity had developed, and soon he and two young Scots, BERT JANSCH and ROBIN WILLIAMSON, started a Folk Club at the Crown Inn, Edinburgh, where Hamish Imlach, Davey Graham, Archie Fisher, Jeanie Robertson, The Corries and folk song-collector Hamish Henderson were regular visitors. After Jansch left to seek his fortune in London, Clive and Robin worked as a duo for some time, making their first recording on a compilation album and then, when Robin went to Morocco, Clive and another Scots musician MIKE HERON opened 'Clive's Incredible Folk Club' in Glasgow. On Robin's return the trio became THE INCREDIBLE STRING BAND and soon impressed record producer Jo Boyd: the resulting LP released on Electra in 1966 was recorded in 7 hours – all first takes!

Shortly after the record's release, Clive left the group to travel overland to India. Legend has it that he collected his royalties and went, but Clive strenuously denies this, saying that "the time was right for a change" and he sees his epic as a voyage of discovery. Returning to England in 1968, Clive followed a friend's recommendation and moved to Cornwall. At this time Henry Bartlett was running the Folk Cottage at Mitchell, which featured a group of talented performers including the young Ralph McTell, 'Whispering' Mick Bennett and local guitarists Pete Berryman, John Bidwell and Tim Wellard. Soon Clive, Henry, Pete and vocalist Jill Johnson formed THE FAMOUS JUG BAND, touring extensively throughout Britain from their Cornish base.

The Famous Jug Band's first LP, dominated by Jill's haunting voice, was recorded in 1969 and featured Clive's classic song *A Leaf Must Fall;* it is now a collector's item, highly regarded by the Folk fraternity. Clive's next group THE STOCKROOM FIVE was a goodtime band playing the footstamping music of American 1930s country star Uncle Dave Macon (Clive banjo, Tim Wellard and John Bidwell guitars, Mick Bennett washboard) and then in 1970 Clive, with John Bidwell and Demelza Val Baker on tablas formed the TEMPLE CREATURES. Heavily influenced by the Indian vogue of the day, the Temple Creatures expressed the inventive talents of Clive and John through a weird collection of instruments including Balalaika, Dulcitar and the Indian hand organ.

The Temple Creatures parted soon after moving to London in 1972 and reformed, with Mick Bennett (vocals /percussion) as CLIVE'S ORIGINAL BAND. C.O.B. did seem for some time destined for success, receiving rave notices in the music press and recording 2 albums of pretty innovative material but, after a major tour as support to Pentangle, finishing at The Royal Festival Hall, the group went their separate ways.

Once again, Clive moved on, this time returning to Cornwall and settling in Penwith where he formed a partnership with poet Bob Devereux creating a stimulating mixture of words and music which they took on tour throughout Devon and Cornwall. In 1978 the duo were joined by Tim Wellard (guitars) and Dick Reynolds (keyboards) to form RHOMBUS who had a brief but memorable career, including a concert with Robin Williamson's Merry Band which was recorded by Radio Berlin.

In recent years Clive has confined himself to the occasional solo performance, concentrating mainly on his enthusiasm for instrument making (Northumbrian, Cornish and Uillean bagpipes and a lute). He does not resent the greater financial success of many of his contemporaries, feeling that his own freedom was much preferable to the nomadic life of the professional musician. Confident that he left the music business at the right time, Clive feels that opportunities for creative acoustic music to be economically viable will only return with the reaction of a new generation against the electronic manipulations of today. Without patronage from disinterested sponsors, music has to be commercial to survive and as long as art and creativity are measured by financial rewards a really creative scene is unlikely – in the end the public is the final judge. Clive Palmer these days plays for himself; his music becomes more refined, his output less, but he seems a contented man.

DISCOGRAPHY

1. Edinburgh Folk Festival Vol. 1 (1965).
2. The Incredible String Band (1966).
3. Sunshine Possibilities—Famous Jug Band (1969).
4. Spirit of Love—C.O.B. (1972).
5. Moishe McStiff—C.O.B. (1974).
6. Suns and Moons—with Bob Devereux (tape, 1978).
7. Just Me — Solo German L.P. (1979).

Molly Parkin

Mike Venning (December 1986)

Image, presence, appearance—Molly Parkin—reginal purple, besequinned and fantastically embroidered, Andrew Logan ring the size of a dustbin-lid and all glittering out from the one tiny figure. Scenario incongruous—small shed/studio at Botallack, an average day, wind gusting and rain never far away. Oh God, standard intro, enough of that, especially as ninety per cent of people I've talked to in Penwith have intimated close friendship or sure knowledge of Molly. Admittedly, the other ten per cent have been totally ignorant of her existence (Jesus, what hole in the ground have they hidden in for the last twenty years?) So let's run a resumé of a multi-faceted life.

Art School—was at Brighton with Mary Quant (senior by three years it seems), then painted successfully in the 'fifties.

Fashion—came up with ideas for Biba and ran a boutique, then was taken on by I.P.C. to be fashion editor of *Nova* magazine. Came up with new ways of portraying fashion (natural-looking models, etc.) and moved on up to the *Sunday Times* where first confronted with the requirement to write. So started with interviews and went on from that.

Novels and St. Ives—chucked *Sunday Times* and met up with Patrick Hughes, moved to St. Ives, stirred up social and artistic scene and began writing novels. Wrote ten, mostly satirically salacious, some of which were belted out in very short times.

New York—changed continent, lived in New York at the Chelsea Hotel (the room where Sid 'n Nancy did themselves in, bloodstains still on the floor)—night-lifestyle—celebrity discoing and all attendant vices, lasted a year by which time found the whole thing not to taste and moved back to Britain.

London/Wales—took to a quieter lifestyle, spent time in native South Welsh valley—back to roots—writing poetry. Offered chance to do one-woman show so did it—instant success—Ronnie Scott's, Edinburgh Festival, touring the country. Recently started work on a large-scale novel based in S.Wales Appeared in a ballet as a Mae-West-style fairy.

Future—maybe a return to painting (retrospective of paintings from long ago coming up in London.)

A lot of activities have been packed in there, and no sign of any slow-down yet. A grandmother next year (someone must have heard that plaintive cry in the Sloop, "The trouble with bringing up liberated daughters is that you've got to wait ten thousand bloody years to become a grandmother!"). I bet that doesn't halt any action either.

Nevertheless, presenting Molly Parkin as all image and no substance would be unjust. OK, she's been so upfront that to many eyes she's seen as a self-publicising, brassy tart with insane clothes who talks dirty. Hidden in that crummy moralising are two important strands of unpleasant social repression. One is male hatred and fear of any successful woman who has the gall to stand up and demonstrate the fact with panache. The other is plain old green-eyed envy, which knows no gender boundaries and whose venom is unhappily increased by the ingredient of self-hatred.

To define where Molly stands I suppose the term 'café society,' without the demeaning connotations that have been attached over the years, is appropriate. I'm thinking of Paris at the turn of the century, when the cafés were filled with an amazing assortment of eccentrics and strong personalities, who were working at the great art, literature and music for which they are remembered, while cavorting and displaying themselves to the often disapproving public gaze of the time. Flamboyance is not necessarily synonymous with empty-headedness, even though British reserve (see previous para—hatred and envy) would like to pin it down as just that.

Now let's wait and see how Molly's *chef-d'oeuvre* turns out. Her previous novels humped the light fantastic while this one recounts South Welsh life over the generations and is being researched and considered without one eye on a deadline. Also her painting: is this a new turn, serious novelist and artist? Why not? It's been a life and a half so far, and you know that whatever Molly Parkin does she'll stand up there with it, taking and loving those slings and arrows of outrageous fortune. Hide her light under a bushel? Not bleedin' likely!

Terry Pascoe

Martin Val Baker (September 1985)

When I called on Cornish illustrator Terry Pascoe a couple of years ago, I was very impressed by his incredibly detailed drawings of Fairy Tale figures set in pastoral backgrounds. Thinking that he would make a good subject for a *Voice* profile, I collected photographer Ashley Peters and headed off for Terry's home at Lowertown just outside Helston, where he lives with artist Sally Cole and their three children. It seems, however, that at the moment he is suffering from the artist's equivalent of 'writer's block' and has been neglecting his drawing in order to create a magnificent garden beside his home—something that would not look out of place in the drawings themselves. As with many other similar talents in Cornwall, the conflict between unrewarded artistic ability and economic survival has taken its toll.

Terry Pascoe was born (1943) and bred in Camborne, coming from mining stock, many of his family having worked at Dolcoath. A 'stuggy little Cornishman,' Terry played rugby for Camborne and Cornwall Colts, for whom he was 'the shortest wing in history'. After schooling in Penzance, Terry was accepted at Falmouth Art School where he specialised in illustration, later moving on to London's Central Art School on an NDD course. After 18 months, the pressures of London life became too much and Terry returned to Cornwall where for the next ten years he earned his living through a long series of labouring, gardening, farming and seasonal jobs, whilst continuing his drawing in the evenings. In 1972 Terry went back to Falmouth Art School to complete a three year BA course which he eventually passed with honours—having had such a long break from formal education Terry managed to persuade the Tutors to come to him while he worked at home. The good grant he received at this time enabled him for once to be free from financial worries and concentrate on his work which included a thesis on Elizabethan miniaturist Nicholas Hilliard.

After finishing Art School, and with an agent's help, quite a bit of work came his way including illustrations for magazines, book covers and also an American Educational book

In 1976 Boondoggle Magazines commissioned Terry to write and illustrate five books for children based on the five traditional fairy families of Cornwall: the Piskies, the Brownies, the Spriggins, the Small People and the Buccas. The first of these, *Daisy and the Small* People was published in Holland (with an English edition due later) and Terry was hard at work on the other books when the publishing company folded up without paying him! Terry's immediate reaction was to go to London to "Duff them up" but he was advised by his solicitors that this was "the worse thing you could do". A chastened man, Terry returned to the rather more mundane world of magazine illustration until he conceived the idea of an illustrated book of medieval ballads. Whilst touting this scheme around the London publishers, Terry encountered the paradox that has haunted his career, "the book people said the work was too like painting and the art people said it was too much like illustration." At last the leading firm of Methuen declared an interest and the proposed book, due out next year, will have twenty full colour illustrations as well as cover and end-papers all by Terry. Featured in the glossy 1977/8 Illustrators' Annual, Terry was invited to a launching for the book at the Ritz Hotel and it was here that he received his favourite press quote when he was described as 'a rough diamond, fresh up from the westcountry with a suit that had not seen the light of day for ten years.'

Asked who had influenced him, Terry immediately named Elvis Presley, Buddy Holly and the Everly Brothers, as he had never really studied other illustrators. He likes to do his drawings in front of the TV or whilst listening to Radio 4 though he finds it difficult to work when other people are in the room. His first sketches are in pencil, then biro and water colours are added with the high-lights done in wash.

As his garden gets bigger and bigger, (and he plans to get some poultry and possibly a pig), I wondered if he will ever have the time to get back to illustration. On the next occasion, I think, we had better send our horticultural expert Old Hodge to see Terry Pascoe, illustrator and gardener!

David Penhaligon

Mike Sagar Fenton (February 1987)

On one of his last visits to my new office he was, as usual, smoking, and I said, "Haven't you seen the no-smoking stickers in the outer office?" "Yes," he said, "but you've got none in here and don't tell me you don't have the odd cigar in here." "Well yes," I said, "but the staff decided when we moved to make it a no-smoking zone so kindly desist."

After our meeting I left him chatting and went into the chamber. When I returned later I saw one of the anti-cigarette stickers on the polished oak of my door.

"Who put that there?" I protested to a chorus of giggles. Then I looked closely. In unmistakable Penhaligon handwriting were the words "Including cigars".

He got the last word.

David Steel, M.P.

"Hello my friend," he said, "I'd have given you a lift up from home if I'd known you were coming." He was up to his elbows in printers' ink and with all his considerable engineering ingenuity at work coaxing a reluctant litho press to produce thousands of last-minute leaflets for the Brecon By-election.

The leaflet was his inspiration—he had spotted that the last-minute survey information pointed to a narrow Liberal victory, so he stuck his message on a piece of paper and got us all delivering it. Two days later he was proved right.

That was the true David Penhaligon: as clever with his hands as he was with his head, as practical as he was political, as good at coaxing a machine as a meeting to respond, and never failing his friends when there was a job to do.

Add to that the sheer enjoyment it was to be with him, and you begin to understand why people of all parties—and of none—feel a personal sense of deep loss...and that his example did much to offset the tarnished reputation of politics and politicians.

Paul Tyler

"Blimey—I can't vote for that, it's like asking turkeys to vote for Christmas."

Quoted by Cyril Smith, M.P.

My favourite Penhaligon remark (for obvious reasons): "When I get into the train at Truro after the next election, I want to know that there are already going to be two Alliance M.P.s in it on the way up to London."

Harold Carter

His practical skills were in much demand and one of his regular "routines" was to tell the story of how he dropped everything on getting an urgent summons to the leader's office only to find when he got there that the secretaries wanted him to fix the coffee machine!

David Steel, M.P.

When I arrived at the House of Commons after the last election, the place was full of Tories. They were sitting on the benches; sitting round the Speaker's chair; squatting on the floor; almost hanging from the gallery. And there we were, about twenty of us facing this blue horde. And one of my new colleagues turned to me and said "You know, David, we've got to ***dominate*** *this Parliament."*

Harold Carter

David was acting as fund-raiser at the Alliance Ball and was trying to auction off a crate of Champagne. He was treating the champagne like an expert auctioneer would handle a heifer at a cattle market. Suddenly, Annette popped up with a bid for £150 and David's face went white. David never drank alcohol! There was a long pause before anyone else came in with another bid to top it, but the relief on David's face was plain to see!

David Owen, M.P.

We were both invited by the chairman of the Central Electricity Generating Board to his office so that he could provide us with the details of the prospective sites the CEGB intended investigating for the purpose of establishing eventually a nuclear power station.

Naturally we both sought details of the precise location. On the wall of the chairman's office was a very large map of the South West Region—I think the scale was six inches to one mile, so that Cornwall was almost at office floor level.

David Penhaligon and myself spent the subsequent ten minutes crawling around on the floor attempting to identify the exact location .

The chairman of the CEGB and his senior managers, who were unaware of the Parliamentary boundary sensitivities concerned, were quite amazed at David and myself crawling around the floor of his office and alternatively issuing expressions of relief or disappointment from our respective positions.

Needless to say David subsequently enjoyed his lunch more than I did!

Robert Hicks, M.P.

He used to print our leaflets in a little shed on his father's caravan site. Breakdowns followed by rapid repairs were the order of the day. Even when all the leaflets were printed all did not always run smoothly. I remember one occasion when ambitiously we planned leaflet drops in Fowey and Flushing on the same day. We sorted the leaflets out and put them in our respective cars. I drove to Fowey, opened the boot and took out—the Flushing leaflets!

Malcolm Brown—Agent

He said that Derek Burrell, who recently retired as Headmaster at Truro School, was showing around a rather posh lady who was thinking of sending her two boys there a few years ago.

At the end of the visit, she said that she understood that Mr. Penhaligon had been educated at the school? "Yes," said Mr. Burrell, rather proudly.

"Well," she retorted, "if my sons come here I want them to leave speaking the Queen's English, unlike ***that*** *man."*

David Harris, M.P.

"I can only describe it as almost an obscene pleasure!" ... on winning the Truro seat for the first time.

We were travelling down to Truro by train. A couple of Canadian tourists became very drunk and rowdy. David endured their behaviour with growing impatience.

One of them asked him a question about something we were passing. "Please excuse my ignorance," the Canadian said.

"I will excuse your ignorance, but not your drunken behaviour" David snapped back.

He lit another cigarette and thought deeply. A minute later. he was back with the Canadians. "I'll forgive your ignorance if you'll excuse my rudeness," he said ... and settled down to a long and friendly chat.

David Mudd, M.P.

CORNISH
TIN
MINERS

Litz Pisk

Pam Otto (July 1986)

Litz Pisk's most recent exhibition was held at the Newlyn Orion in April and May of this year but her drawings have been shown in Vienna and London since 1933. There have been two solo exhibitions of her work at the New Art Centre during the '80s and one held at the Redfern in 1944. One would think this added up to a fruitful and satisfying career as an artist but that is in fact only half of her story. For the subject matter of her drawings is the body in movement, and this is Litz Pisk's other love in life.

As a child she and her brother both suffered from a spinal problem and, by way of correction, were taken to classes with Elizabeth Duncan, sister to Isadora. It was from these classes and the philosophy behind them that one suspects Litz began her fascination with movement and to formulate her own philosophy and her study of the language of body movement. In her home town of Vienna she studied architecture of the theatre and Kinnetism at art school. At the end of her studies she was asked to do the designs for a Kurt Weill and Berthold Brecht production of 'The Rise and Fall of the Town Mahogany,' which was a great success. This led to her first exhibition of drawings, of which an art critic of the time said "movement is of great interest to her and she succeeds to characterise a human being with a few movement lines."

In 1933, when she first came to England, there was nobody who had even considered the necessity of movement classes for actors, which these days is almost unthinkable. The cultural upheavals which were going on, not only in Europe but all over the world, particularly in the theatre world, was the new and rich diet that Litz Pisk brought to R.A.D.A. when she started working there. Inevitably people began to feel that a whole new concept of teaching drama needed to be evolved and consequently a group of her friends, led by the brilliant Michel St. Denis, got together to discuss just such a project, which led to the opening of the London Old Vic Theatre School. This school produced actors and actresses, directors and stage managers who comprise some of the best in the theatre today. The school's profound effect on contemporary theatre has gone almost unnoticed and the people, including Litz Pisk, who conceived and executed these changes are as yet unrecognised for their enormous contributions.

Litz went on, later in life, to teach at the Bath Academy of Art and at the Central in London, continually learning and refining her methods of teaching. During the war, she found herself involved with a motley crew of war orphans, who she says were her greatest teachers. One senses that this was an intensely happy and fulfilling time for her and that she loved working with the children. In fact she enjoyed the work so much that even when she was again working full time at the Old Vic Theatre School she still spent every weekend with the children at their school in Cambridge.

She told us a delightful story of a child who had drawn a house in one of the art classes and had painted green smoke coming out of the chimney. The child next to him protested, saying that smoke should be grey. The house-drawer replied very crossly that it was green because his mother was cooking spinach in the kitchen. This story echoes her own theories on movement quite succinctly. She said once "Ariel need not fly if his form contains the experience of flight."

Part of her classes with actors involved a term-long study of an animal of their choice. The point was not to imitate the animal but to come to a clear understanding of 'what made it tick' and then to find that inside oneself. It is an exacting technique and I imagine that Litz Pisk, who gives so much of herself to whatever task is at hand, would have had little time for those students who didn't give of their all. She wrote in her book, "Freely give from the abundance of your existence to the vitality of the theatre." There is no doubt that this is just what Litz Pisk has done throughout her life with single-mindedness and clarity. Litz has had a distinguished and perhaps exhausting career from which she is now taking a well-earned rest away from the public eye. She lives in a beautiful and remote cottage set in dramatic surroundings, almost theatrical in dimension, where she continues to explore her fascination with the reproduction of the moving body in line. Listening to her talking about her work I was reminded of the old Haiku masters of Japanese poetry who, through a strict adherence to a precise form and a paring down of all inessentials, strove to arrive at universal truth. To an outsider, to me anyway, this kind of achievement amounts to a kind of magic, or alchemy and I came away feeling that Litz Pisk was a wizard of a woman.

Maddy Prior

Martin Val Baker (September 1990)

Photo: Maddy with Rick Kemp

Maddy Prior, lead singer with top folk band Steeleye Span; came to The Acorn, Penzance, earlier this month (with husband Rick Kemp) to give two sell-out performances. *Voice* took the opportunity to snatch a quick interview between gigs.

MVB. Did you have any *early musical influences? The Weavers, Joan Baez?*
MP. There was never a lot of music around our home. My father wrote and the last thing he wanted was noise. I've always been quiet around the house, I never put music on or sing to myself. I got involved in performing when the boy I was going out with was asked to play guitar in a group and he agreed on condition that I could sing with them. I found the club system with resident spots and guest appearances a bit weird. No dancing! I thought this was a very bizarre way to carry on—I was used to go out bopping for four hours. It took me a long time to get into English music at all.

You never learned an instrument?
I had a go on banjo, I had a go on guitar, harp ... practically everything ... but never stuck to it, I haven't got the tenacity. I did about a year on my own on the club circuit and then teamed up with Tim Hart, who was also from St Albans. The only work I've ever done apart from singing was a week in a Wimpy Bar at Torquay. After that I decided to stick to music. I was driving a couple of Americans around and they told me to stop singing American songs "because it sounds abysmal" and to learn some English material. They played me *a* load of tapes; at first it sounded awfully dull but gradually I got to like them and realised that it would be a better idea to do English songs.

How do you feel about new arrangements of the old songs? There's an argument that the modern arrangements make them easier to listen to...
I think it does make them more accessible to some people—it's not always easy to listen to an old boy singing. Often, though, the researchers caught the end of these people's singing lives. They would have been very much more impressive as young singers. There's a tendency to think that the late recordings are the way it's supposed to be, but it's not necessarily so. As young people, they would have had very strong voices generally speaking, you don't get up and sing unless you have a good voice.

So the arrangements by Steeleye, Fairport, Pentangle and the others have made traditional music more attractive to the general listener?
We're used to hearing harmonic music with chords, basically because we're used to hearing American music. English music is totally alien to the English; on the whole they find it very strange and dull and the drone they can't cope with at all, because they are more familiar with American music. Putting chords behind English songs gives them a route map to what the song is about.

It's a musical language that they understand ...
One they are more familiar with, certainly, but we don't do it for that reason—we just liked the songs and wanted to make them more acces-sible for us, never mind the rest of the world!

When did you start writing songs yourself?
Much later; I never really wrote with Steeleye but when the band split up for a couple of years I did a solo album and also wrote most of the material for the Maddy Prior Band. Rick and I write most of our material together.

Do you still enjoy touring?
I quite like travelling, though it's harder at the moment, being away from the children. As long as the tour is not too massive ... I get a bit bored.

Can you now ration yourselves ... do the ones you want to?
We tend to take certain periods of time, which is a better way of doing it.

Steeleye Span, Maddy Prior Band, Silly Sisters, Maddy and Rick ... are there any other combinations?
The Carnival Band; we've done an album of carols Tapestry of Carols, and three Christmas tours.

Is it mainly a vocal group?
No, it's double bass, percussion, fiddle, recorders, clarinet, shauns ... from early music to Cajun. We've just done an album of hymns called *Sing Lustily with Good Courage.* It's a great Christmas tour, very jolly. We do the shortest pantomime in the world—just the plot.

On stage, do you feel you can control or manipulate an audience?
No!

Every night it's a challenge?
Oh yes. If we had an 'act' as such it would be very boring—it's not what I've ever worked at or done. You fall into doing certain things because they relate to the songs, but generally speaking we vary the show quite a lot because it has to be real on the night, particularly with Rick and I.

But what gets a good performance—is it a particular audience, a particular day you've had?
I've no idea. Quite often one of us thinks it's a good performance and the other doesn't; sometimes half the audience thinks it's great and half thinks it rotten.

Can you tell from the applause?
I've given up trying to guess—I just go out and do it! I remember once that one of the audience was not clapping at all and I wondered why he had bothered to come. What was the point of him being there if he was not happy? Yet, at the end, he came up to me and said that the show was absolutely wonderful! I can never judge what's on the mind of an audience. Some people laugh in a crowd, some leg it mentally ... some don't seem to respond but explode at the end. Audiences don't think they can be seen!

There's a different etiquette for different sorts of music.
Yes, and they're not quite sure what it's supposed to be with us.

If you had to be judged on one album, which would it be?
I couldn't really say, because each one has two or three tracks that I particularly like; but it can be different for the other musicians—some numbers are better live than recorded and vice versa I did like Parcel of Rogues though; we did a lot of strong Jacobite material.

Any new projects?
Well, there's the Carnival Band album, Steeleye have an album out and continue to tour intermittently. People are always asking if the band have finished but it carries on with a 'low media profile'.

It's like an old firm that's been going on for ....
Twenty-one years! It's a smashing band now and is moving faster than it has for ten years. We have Liam Genockey on drums, Tim Harris on bass, Peter Knight on fiddle and Bob Johnson on guitar. We had an album out last year called *Tempted and Tried.* Rick and I have *Happy Families* out in October which reflects the work we are doing together.

If you ever come off the road can you see yourself doing anything else? Could you perhaps, like your father, write prose or plays?
I haven't got the stamina for it!

So you'll keep on singing till the end...?
I think so, yes.

Roy Ray

Sue Monro (April 1983)

To many people, the word 'artist' is synonymous with a certain way of life ... either that of the inebriate degenerate or the eccentric elitist, divorced from the realities of everyday life. Roy Ray is neither of these: he adheres to a strong work ethic and painting is an integral part of existing in the real world of earning a living and supporting his family. His average working day starts at 7.30a.m in his studio at the St. Ives School of Painting and finishes when energy levels sink to zero at the end of the day ... not quite a workaholic artist, but he does admit to needing the steady influence of a regular work routine. Perhaps this down-to-earth attitude has its roots in Roy's London working-class background; It certainly works well for him. His paintings, with their strong local references and mystical overtones, are now recognised alongside the work of Wynter, Lanyon and Nicholson. He has exhibited extensively in the South West and his paintings are well represented in private collections all over the world.

The Cornish Connection

Roy has drawn and painted for most of his life, initially without commitment or formal training. It wasn't until 1976 that he became totally immersed in his work His early involvement with landscape was based on conventional impressionism but, after moving to Cornwall in 1973, he became increasingly frustrated with the limitations this style imposed, he recalls ... "it's geology, archaeology, weather, the massive forces of nature so evident in winter and, above all, the beautiful eroded textures and muted colours ... the need to express something of all these aspects led me to look beyond conventional figurative painting." Two new aspects emerged as part of the move towards abstraction ... the aerial perspective and the introduction of collage.

The Aerial Perspective

A chance flight in an aircraft from St. Just in 1979 marked the most significant event in his artistic career ... "at that moment everything changed; from 1000ft. I saw a landscape without space, rendered flat; no horizon, no top or bottom, just texture and colour." Three years' dilemma, the opposing forces of realism and abstraction had been resolved. Man's dream of emulating birds in flight has been a source of inspiration for many painters.... The elimination of representational subject matter or its distortion beyond recognition creates a stimulating new vision. Man's worst offences are aesthetically upgraded ... the automobile scrapyard is transformed into an attractive multi-coloured design. Yet the elevated viewpoint does not create space only surfaces, perhaps the key to an optical code as a shortcut to oneself... Roy's landscapes are not only concerned with topographical features but can also be comprehended as a surface built up or eroded through vast periods of time, almost as if he is plumbing the earth's secret depths and exploring his own heart of creation.

Techniques and Interpretations

The introduction of collage gave Roy the perfect medium to illustrate and convey more fully the textures, colours and depths inherent in the Cornish landscape. He uses fine layers of tissue paper and gauze, primed with acrylic and gesso which form interlocking shapes that can be interpreted in many ways, laterally as torsos, crumbling stone walls, coastal prominences or vertically as flat mandalas. A stone circle set in natural earthy colours becomes interchangeable with a transverse section from a lump of granite. Infinitely subtle colour/tone variations suggest seasonal changes, alternating weather conditions and add a touch of realism. For Roy there is also a mysterious element in painting ... he finds a spontaneous touchstone emerges from an unplanned shape even though the colours and overall feeling of the painting were worked out in advance. This element of surprise runs through all his work ... occasional word/letter configurations become textural devices that enhance the overall surface effect ... they assume an enigmatic character when stripped of literary meaning, yet they are arranged with careful regard to the environmental balance and aesthetic well-being of the overall surface. This juxtaposition of soft colours, horizontal lines, undulating circles with scraps of text stimulates different parts of the brain simultaneously, yet the over-all effect is one of elegance and harmony. Perhaps his paintings reflect a subconscious need to get back to the pure, simple fundamentals that have been eroded by the complexities of present day life, in the sense that our environment is becoming uncontrollable; at least the artist can feel safe in a world of colour and texture that is within his control. We all draw on our own experience of life when we view the work of another painter; I found Roy Ray's paintings function on many different levels, even though he is primarily concerned with landscape.

Words and Music

Roy finds painting absorbs most of his time and energy and gives full expression to his personality but this doesn't exclude appreciation and participation in other creative fields. As well as talking with energy and humour, he also listens to music whilst painting; the long drawn out sounds of Tangerine Dream, Nordic instrumental music and Sibelius echo his own feelings towards the Penwith landscape. He also finds time to travel around the country giving lectures on the work of other St. Ives artists. He is presently working with Bob Devereux on two different projects ... one long-standing ambition, to publish an historical analysis of the work of all the major St. Ives artists, plus a stage performance involving poetry, music and narrative based on the life and work of Borlase Smart.

In addition to fostering new developments in abstract painting, Roy is also a lively and vigorous teacher. Since 1976 he has run the St Ives School of Painting; he loves working with other people and sees no conflict in teaching traditional painting skills whilst continuing to develop his own unique style. He is a member of both the Newlyn and Penwith Societies of Artists and organises exhibitions for the Penwith Gallery. It is clear that this artist, with his finely tuned sensibility, sheer joy in the creative process and personal relationship with his natural environment, will produce many good pictures in the future.

John Renbourn

Martin Val Baker (February 1990)

Voice: What do you think of Jacqui McShee?

JR: This is the first couple of gigs we've done for some time. We don't work regularly now so for me it's a great pleasure, wonderful. We first worked together in the very early 'sixties when I was at Kingston Art School. There was an old boat, Kingston Folk Barge, where I used to play. Jacqui turned up with a guy called Chris Ayliffe. They'd been busking in Paris together and he's never really forgiven me for stealing her away.

Voice: You worked as a duo then?

JR: I think I was already living up in town with Bert and working out some ideas with him—it was at the time the Cousins Club got going. I used to play there with Jacqui and Bert sometimes. Danny Thompson and Terry Cox would drop in from Ronnie Scotts Club to play, so we met them and got the band together.

They were from the jazz world really?

Terry and Danny were working with Alexis Korner at the time, a killer blues trio. It was really fantastic. Danny's stuff was the best; it was just after Blues Incorporated.

Back to the present, you've just finished a tour with Stefan Grossman?

We've done two weeks of travelling around England—first time he's been over for a long time. He's moved back to New York from Italy, and is much happier.

Is he related to Albert Grossman?

No, but he is related to Steve Grossman, who used to work with Miles Davis. Just incidentally, there's a great transvestite drag act called Stevie Grossman and frequently on tour with Stefan you get bunches of flowers sent to the dressing room for the wrong guy with lovely messages! *Can you see yourself working with Bert again?*

It would be great to work with Bert again. It would be wonderful if it did happen; we'd go back to where it started and maybe build it up again.

But you can't go on doing the same old thing. Isn't it tempting to work with younger musicians? While you are working with your own generation all the time, all these kids are coming through.

An interesting point. I'm working at Dartington now and what comes out of the practice rooms now is great, all seventeen year olds. I've already filched a few musicians from there and maybe there'll be more. I don't think it's to do with age so much as with how you get on with people, how you travel together and so on.

Would you rather work with a good musician or a friendly person?

At a certain level musicians mellow out when they've done a certain amount. Often the best players are easy-going people and the ones with a chip on their shoulders maybe don't play that well. The greatest musician I've ever worked with is Tony Roberts, I've worked with him since the 'sixties. It's not that he's a flute player, it's just that his ideas about music eclipse mine totally. He's a beautiful player—and he's a lot older than me! It's not to do with age, it's to do with something else. There was a review in *Folk Roots* saying: "Who is Tony Roberts, he must be the up and coming musician from the new generation."

What about other musical styles, the World Music explosion? A lot of British musicians are wary of acts coming in from abroad, forgetting that British musicians have been touring abroad anyway. Have you been listening to African or Indian music ... any of these new things?

It's not all that new! It explains a lot about this century that a lot of this stuff is now much more available; it's opened up a whole new thing in music.

Do you take the trouble to go and see it or do you hear things by accident?

No; if I'm on tour, maybe I'll catch a band once in a while. If I'm at home, I get the feet up and that's it!

Bert was saying—and Jacqui, too—that they go to watch friends play mainly.

That's right. The African stuff is coming through the record companies, Danny Thompson has a Kora player working with him. I was up in Sweden recently and there was one there and of course there's the ethno musicology courses at Dartington... It's staggering, really, a lot of the tribal music is extraordinary. I heard a tape I couldn't even identify; it sounded like two ocarina players playing the same cyclic five notes against each other, like a rippling banjo pattern—really beautiful. It turned out it was two women singing and using each other's mouths as resonating chambers—wonderful. The guy who does the stuff on African music says that you can't use the term 'African,' there's just so many different types of music.

In fact, the last number you and Jacqui did at the concert had very repetitive rhythms, almost mesmeric.

There you are, strophic, like the kora music, some of it. I had a tune on my last record, an English harpsichord piece. It's got an ostinato bass that just goes between two tonic dominant harmonies and there is a beautiful modal melody. So this African guy played exactly the same changes and used the same scale—you could have superimposed the two things. I was sitting there and I could hear that harpsichord tune!

Daniel Rovai

Martin Val Baker (May 1986)

Daniel Rovai, the French Cabaret performer and Clown, (who spent several years based in the county, first with Footsbarn, and then with his own spectacular offshoot, The Barneys) returned to tour Cornwall recently. After the show in Penzance, he talked to the Voice about his life as a travelling performer.

Daniel was born in Corsica, though the family (he has four brothers) moved to Paris when he was two. There was no theatrical tradition in his family, they were "purely working class," but Daniel himself developed an interest in the craft at an early age. By the age of fifteen, he had left home to travel "as a beatnik" throughout France to discover "the cultural and political currents of my country," and soon found himself involved in travelling Theatre groups and Circuses—at one time working as a stunt rider. It was at this time that he learnt the circus skills that have become his trademark, sometimes paid, sometimes not and often working for just food and accommodation—he was "a young traveller seeking adventure and experience." The 1968 upheaval in Paris, "Our wonderful '68 revolution that ended so badly when everyone went back home and watched colour TV" saw Daniel working with various radical theatre groups in the capital. In the early 'seventies there was a determined attempt to decentralise and popularise the Paris Theatre and the radical groups moved into the suburbs playing to workers in factories. However the experiment failed as the productions became more and more intellectual, eventually drawing their audiences from the centre of Paris and losing popular support.

In 1975 Daniel moved to England where he worked as a solo busker "making a fortune on the streets of Portobello" and then as part of a duo he took a show around England, arriving at last in Cornwall to find that exciting company Footsbarn well established. For three years Daniel worked with Footsbarn performing in the village halls of Cornwall and at venues all over Europe. In 1978 with Margaritte Biereye and musicians Thom Podgoresky and Pete Berryman (a Frenchman, a German, an American and a Cornishman!) he started The Barneys cabaret troupe as an offshoot of the main Footsbarn company, making their debut at the first St. Ives Festival, with 'the Chainbreakers.' It was this group that established Daniel's reputation as an exciting innovator and The Barneys took the Cornish and European circuit by storm, playing at festivals in Zurich, France, Denmark and, of course, the 'Festival of Fools' at Amsterdam. In two years Daniel made enough contacts to keep him going for the next seven.

After Margaritte left to rejoin Footsbarn, Daniel kept the basic Barney format going and over the years has used around 30 different actors and musicians in his group. Just recently, however, he has stopped using the name 'Barneys' preferring to go out under the name 'Daniel Rovai and friends' a title that gives him more freedom to improvise both with show and personnel. If a good booking came up Daniel could take a company of thirty on the road, though the economics dictate that he himself has to guarantee rehearsal and performance fees, a risky business when cancellations can wreak havoc with ingoings. At the moment (apart from an agent who handles TV and Film work) Daniel deals with all the group's administration and finds this an increasing strain. Arts Council money has never come his way and he feels disinclined to spend precious time lobbying for it, preferring instead to get his show on the road and do his job as a performer.

In London, Daniel still does a bit of busking but confines his club appearances to 25-minute spots so as not to get over-exposed. There is some TV work, including TVAM and a good chance of some appearances on the Rory Bremner Show. He was offered 'Saturday Live' but turned it down—"too much of a Pot Pourri," though his big ambition is to play that other Corsican exile Napoleon Bonaparte on the screen, and his agent has approached the directors of two forthcoming 'Napoleonic' productions. Fame, he is happy to wait for, "if it comes too quickly you have to cope with it for the rest of your life—there is plenty of work around to do." Challenge, however, is what he seeks and he would like to do a spell with a major touring company where he could give his maximum as an actor and not have to worry about the day to day administration of his own group. He is gradually becoming more choosy about the solo and group bookings that he does take but is always happy to come back to Cornwall where he has a strong affection for the "artistic current and the countryside."

Venues are becoming more of a problem, even in Europe the Arts are in crisis, but Daniel finds the situation particularly bad in Britain and feels that the sponsoring authorities should put more money into venues and organisations so that the artistes themselves can be promoted properly. In Europe there is a tradition of Café Theatre with which there is no parallel in this country; the Arts Centre format here tends to discourage audiences and they should be made more informal and adaptable rather than places where people go to "consume Art." In Europe Daniel finds that people are more aware of the requirements of artistes, "when you get a good reception there is a 100% chance of a good performance" but in Britain lack of proper facilities often means that actors go on stage disadvantaged from the start.

With Arts Council funding Daniel would love to work in Cornwall for a spell, feeling that there are a lot of talented performers in the county who could perhaps be gathered together for one big production. He has in fact offered a mammoth show to this year's Elephant Fayre and one can only hope that the organisers will have the courage to give Daniel Rovai his chance; it is unlikely that the less imaginative Arts Association would feel able to.

"When you get to my age, you realise that everyone else has a family, a house and a bank account—I'm still on the road: if I break a leg or get a chest infection, I would end up in hospital with absolutely nothing behind me" : Daniel Rovai.

Lord St. Levan

Greg Palmer (August 1990)

St Michael's Mount—Ictis to the ancients—a port of commerce in antiquity, a Celtic temple during the first millennium, monastery and occasional fortress (the monks had to put up with it) until Henry VIII's disagreement with Anne Boleyn, fortress until the end of the English Civil War, when Colonel John St Aubyn (one of Cromwell's men) was appointed Governor of The Mount. He became a strong supporter of the restoration of King Charles II after Cromwell's death. It has remained the St Aubyn's family home right through to the present day. Lord St Levan took over the Mount in 1978.

As Peters and I gasp and wheeze our way up the cobbled path toward the summit of St Michael's Mount, we ponder, as so many visitors do, on the possible existence of a secret helicopter landing pad, tucked away on the seaward side of the crag for the personal use of John St Aubyn, the Fourth Lord St Levan. He is, the Mount Guides insist, a fit and active man of seventy-one and negotiates the steep climb several times daily, though he did succumb to the pleasures of a golfing buggy for a while, after he had hurt his back.

We turn, as instructed, off the Pilgrims' Steps, ancient trail to the summit since the Mount became a holy place after the appearance of The Archangel to some fishermen in AD495, and head for the door at the East Wing where, we've been told, the Houseman awaits us. This is the private part of the castle, the Victorian wing, the St Levans' inner sanctum.

There is a model of the Mount on public display, constructed by a former butler to the St Aubyn family, which has been carved entirely out of champagne corks. This is a testament both to the number of fish courses served at the time and to the bleak isolation of the Cornish winter, exacerbated by the remoteness of the castle from the mainland.

We are ushered into The Snuggery, a rectangular room with two octagonal ante-rooms with panoramic views across Mounts Bay. Today is a charity day, one of twenty-five in the season, when the day's entire take on the gate is donated to one of the many charities of which the St Levans are patrons. In one of the ante-chambers, members of The Fisherman's Mission, Newlyn, are taking tea. The atmosphere is intimate and we feel like intruders. Lady St Levan, sensing our distress after the long climb, makes us welcome and offers us coffee, which we try not to slurp down too greedily . . .

Lord St Levan takes leave of his guests and sits with us on the sofas around the fireplace. He is a man of considerable personal charm and dryness of wit, with a reputation as a raconteur after the dinner plates have been cleared.

He was, he says, born in London, though "God knows where". He adds mysteriously that his father was in the Grenadier Guards. He then went on to Eton and Cambridge, where he gained a degree in law. Money was in short supply, the then John St Aubyn had four other siblings, and his education had to be paid for by a wealthy uncle.

Lord St Levan's ancestor, the Fifth Baronet, was a flamboyant figure by all accounts and, as well as fathering fifteen illegitimate children, gambled away the family fortune in the casinos of London. He is reputed to have hidden inside a chimney to escape the attentions of his angry creditors, whilst the maid walked up and down in front of the fireplace to obscure his exposed foot! When he died much of the family's art collection had to be sold off to pay for his excesses.

Before the last war, John St Aubyn trained as an agricultural labourer, schooled in the knowledge that he would one day take over the family estate. "I milked the cows, and I buried the dead sheep," he says wryly. Part of his life at that time involved working in the hop gardens of Kent as a 'hop-measurer'.

"That's all finished ... those marvellous people from the East End! And I had to measure the hops, and get sworn at by these East End ladies!"

Soon after this came a career in the Royal Navy Voluntary Reserve in which he served as a Lieutenant on a minesweeper. After leaving on one of the Russian convoys he spent a considerable part of the war helping to keep the ports of Murmansk and Archangel free for shipping.

Asked whether he enjoyed his wartime days, Lord St Levan smiles and says, "It was jolly cold and jolly dangerous, too. Minesweeping was very dangerous because, if you were tracked by an aeroplane, by the time you'd cut yourself free of your mineweeping gear, the aeroplane had dropped its bombs ... or the submarine had fired its torpedoes."

Lord St Levan chuckles again and adds, "Of course, one of the advantages of being on a minesweeper is that you didn't have to kill anyone!"

After the war he was given his own command, HMS *Prospect*, and took charge of escorting German ships loaded with nerve gas which were then sunk off the south coast of Norway.

In 1948 he qualified as a solicitor and entered general practice. John St Aubyn went on to live in London during its infamous 'swinging' heyday. (He married very late in life, at the age of fifty.) He recalls his first criminal case, that of defending a hoodlum who made the mistake of shooting a policeman. This was in the days when the rope was in vogue, but the man concerned lived to serve a nine-year sentence.

Lord St Levan remembers Ruth Ellis the last woman to be hanged in Great Britain. "I knew her, poor girl. Crime of passion! She was a barmaid in a club, a very attractive girl. I felt very sorry for her because she ... she was treated rather badly by her boyfriend. So she shot him."

During the 'sixties, John St Aubyn, though continuing his work as a solicitor, opened the first launderettes in London. "Nobody had heard of them before ... in Clapham and the Old Kent Road."

Another business venture was in slot-TV rental, electrical repair and selling pies to Australians in South Kensington. The TV business continues to prosper to this day with outlets throughout Cornwall and he still acts for himself as a solicitor.

Lord St Levan sits in the House of Lords but scorns the idea of taking a party whip and declares emphatically "I'm an Independent like any true Cornishman!"

In the House of Lords, he reserves his energies for issues of which he has a specialist knowledge: "In the House of Lords, if you're going to make a speech, you'd better make damn sure you know your subject."

John St Aubyn takes his title from the village of St Levan just south of Land's End. "The first Lord St Levan was a Liberal member of the House of Commons. He used to buy his fish-bait for his yacht from Mousehole. Then Mousehole voted Tory. He despaired about that, so he then bought his fishbait from St Levan down the coast because they'd voted Liberal. Otherwise, I'd have been Lord Mousehole!"

Lord St Levan has no direct heir and the Mount and title will go to his nephew, James St Aubyn (elder brother of Nicholas St Aubyn, PPC for the Conservatives), thus ending a charming if somewhat confusing tradition of every heir holding the Christian name of 'John '.

Amy Scofield

Sue Monro (July 1983)

By its nature, a piece of jewellery is precious, .not only in its intrinsic value as gold, silver or gems but also because of its smallness and the delicacy of its design and workmanship. Being small, it invites close scrutiny as well as a desire to touch and savour its form and surface. Amy Scofield's jewellery has all these qualities plus much more ... there's wit, humour, ambiguity and a new dimension in design, in fact it's full of surprises.

Amy has been producing fine pieces of jewellery since the early '70s. It was the need to do something personally creative as a full-time activity (and money earner), whilst living on a boat that provided the initial impetus. She found a teacher through the I.L.E.A. adult education scheme and set about mastering design and technique. But most of what Amy knows about jewellery she has discovered herself through experimentation and hard work. She has been forced to improvise through lack of funds for precision equipment, yet in the hands of an innovator, for whom work is a form of meditation, it is possible to overcome technical limitations and produce intricate, complex works of art.

Amy's jewellery demonstrates how objects taken out of context can become completely satisfying images once the eye is trained to see the specific and to abstract from it the general ... it can never be without stimuli, imagination becomes unlimited, as in her beautifully worked overhead views of rooms, gardens and landscapes in polished silver. Even a standard bathroom is transformed into a fascinating 3 dimensional puzzle ... part optical illusion created by skilled design. Her more abstract designs that show simultaneous views from top, bottom, sides, often with the added dimension of a view through a window reorganise reality in a way that is both stunning and totally original ... yet there is nothing trite or extreme about them, simply because Amy retains the essential truth of the original form. Topographical details inspired by the Cornish landscape, fields, hedges, valleys, trees in total or in part all possess a rich positive/negative interplay, light, dark exchanges and varied surface textures. She strikes a fine balance between simple natural forms, shapes and delicate textural detail ... it compels us to look at the ordinary with 'new' eyes and discover an ever fascinating variety of new shapes and dimensions. Amy's unique designs are a result of her own all-consuming curiosity about the nature of all things. They enable us to see into through and around the mask of fixed reality, stripping away one illusion, sometimes replacing it with another ... every piece shows a fresh approach and functions on different levels. Visually they are a joy to look at and added to that they stimulate the imagination of the beholder.

Amy has exhibited at the Unikat Gallery in Hamburg and at the Newlyn Orion. She sells some of her work on a private commission basis and through retail outlets on S.O.R. She likes to keep her prices as low as possible.

Over the past five years Amy has also been writing poetry, culminating in a book, *Maze*, written last summer which she hopes to have published when the illustrations have been completed. Just as she creates landscapes of the imagination in silver, she is also a powerful sorceress with words. Her writing is closely linked to the evolution of her own inner creative workings. *Maze* is a combination of poetry and prose, loosely connected by some zany narrative passages which give us some idea of the outer lives of the characters; they in their turn serve to enhance and provide a pivoting point for the poetry ... their to and fro banter, vivid witticisms and observations are vehicles for the play of phenomena and the imaginative experience.

To a certain extent, Amy presents us with a child-like vision of the world, where fairies are as real as anything else is and although a child would happily identify with some of the poetry by breaking through surface facilities, this conveys the rhythm and unpretentious language of a living speech ... words flow spontaneously even though she has placed them carefully in specific rhythm patterns: they change according to mood ... sometimes mysterious, sometimes hilarious, always harmonious, succinct, acute and affectionate. The characters and incidental details are imaginary but feelings expressed in the poetry are absolutely true and very much on the side of life ... on the side of potential for happiness, inner growth and fulfilment. This testament is dramatised with occasional flashes of mock tragedy and humour which serve to highlight the sparkle in other passages.

> A funny thing happened on
> the way to the crematorium.
> Trees swayed in the wind
> Birds swooped like maniacs
> Curtains tore across the sky
> And all time was seen in the
> eye of a daisy
> And a cow looked over the
> hedge and spoke:
> "Life is a free gift'"
> And the corpse rose out of its
> coffin and joked,
> "Not to-day, thankyou. I've
> had one."

If prose is the language of common conversation and poetry the noble and sublime way of expressing one's thoughts, Amy combines both styles with great skill. Sadly I can't recommend you to any bookshop that sells her work as she is still searching for a publisher. One hopes her unique talent as a writer will be given the recognition it obviously deserves.

Mike Shepherd

Martin Val Baker (March 1990)

For ten years now Kneehigh Theatre, based in the St Austell area, have been working hard to fill the gap left when the legendary Footsbarn moved to the Continent in 1979. Following the Footies' tradition of playing village halls, as well as getting involved with local communities, Kneehigh's reputation has been steadily growing, culminating in a remarkable series of sell-out performances of *Tregeagle* at the clifftop Minack Theatre. Co-founder of Kneehigh, Mike Shepherd, in Penzance with their Christmas show, talked to the *Voice* about the way things have been going.

Though originally from London Mike has spent most of his life in Cornwall. except for a spell at college, and then as a secondary school drama teacher in the capital. He had no formal drama training but had always been interested in the theatre and, in the 'seventies, was part of the County Council's 'Drama in Education' team along with Shiva's David Hughes and some of Footsbarn. In fact, it was David Hughes who lured Mike back to Cornwall in 1980 with the offer of work with Shiva Theatre in their productions that summer, *Meryasek, Absent Friends* and *The Lion in Winter*—a mixed bag if ever there was one!

During Mike's absence in London, the County Drama Adviser had left and was not replaced, "The whole County Drama Department had gone down the drain, leaving no provision for drama-based work in Cornwall." This, coupled with the loss of Footsbarn, provided the stimulation for Mike Shepherd and a group of actors and musicians based around Mevagissey to create a new theatre company, Kneehigh. In the beginning the company used to "eat, sleep, play and work together. The dynamics and energy came from this," but eventually as the years passed by people got fed up with that and started having families and leading much more separate lives.

Whilst understanding that people mature and move on Mike feels strongly that the moving apart can diffuse the "150% commitment and energy that is needed in this current climate to survive as a struggling small-scale theatre company." In fact, he is now worried that the original 'community' structure of Kneehigh is being reduced to "an administration with a director and short-term contract performers." This, he feels, damages the chances of the company developing any 'House Style' and, although there is still a core of people who have been with Kneehigh for some years, the economic realities of being based in the extreme southwest makes it difficult to keep actors.

Kneehigh's early material came mainly from inside the company, though they often took popular titles and did their own versions of shows like *Jungle Book* or *Around* the *World in 80 Days,* the aim being to get children and their families through the doors to enjoy the performance.

However, as the company came under the eye of the Regional Arts Association and the carrot of funding was dangled; they were encouraged to break new ground and work with writers. "Suddenly the work we were doing, delighting family audiences in village halls in Cornwall, was not good enough for us to be one of their clients, to wave the flag for them around the South West."

For a time, they worked with Jon Oram the mime artist and SWA's Theatre Worker: "As it happened that was a very good move and provided us with a good strong outside eye." Mike is, though aware of the dangers of taking on unsuitable material to humour their funders and the company tries desperately not to get involved with people who are not familiar with the history of the. company. The production of *Cyberg,* for instance, was a classic example: "An innovative piece of work, a very strong piece of theatre that went down very well in specialised venues throughout the country, but was totally irrelevant for the kind of audience we had built up in Cornwall and it lost us a lot of friends."

"If SWA funded a company specifically as an innovative company it would be different, but there doesn't seem to be a priority to produce new work—the recent upping of cash from the Arts Council to SWA has led to more funding of the Theatre Royal for shows like *South Pacific!"*

Like Footsbarn before them, Kneehigh have been travelling in Europe. Each summer they go to Holland and Germany to make money to supplement their work in Cornwall. On the Continent they get proper fees and proper hospitality. One festival they play at in Holland is funded a third by local government, a third by national government, and a third by a local brewery. Admission is free and everyone from Footsbarn and Curtis Mayfield to Spanish and Italian companies are there.

One important aspect of Kneehigh's work in Cornwall is the Community Play, a theatrical experience very much involving local participants. These have been staged in St Ives, Mousehole and Mevagissey. "This sort of work is so important It's low profile, it's not prestigious, it's just very valid and valuable we'd like to be able to do more of it."

In Mevagissey, the project involved not only school children, but also local fishermen (one of whom was persuaded to take the lead part), the village choir, a baker (who provided 700 pastry fishes for the audience) and a 16 foot mermaid specially built for the occasion by Kneehigh Theatre.

In 1989, the company revived *Tregeagle*, a show based on Cornish legend with which they toured the village halls a few years ago. Directed by Mike Shepherd, it was considered to be the most impressive production by Kneehigh to date and, aided by spectacular weather, had a sell-out run at The Minack. The frustrations of trying to keep such a strong cast together are implied by the fact that only two of that cast remain with Kneehigh

With several new players, the company are on the road again with a new show, *The Last Voyage of Long John Silver* an original adaptation of the *Treasure Island* story. "It resulted from a strong request by the people who book us for a show that they could sell to the public—they don't have guarantees against loss any more and can't afford to take any risks They want a family show, a recognisable title, Shakespeare or something from the school syllabus, so they can pack in the school parties."

As always, music is an important part of the show The company has a policy of hiring actor/musicians and building productions around these individual skills. Kneehigh are looking forward to adapting *Long John* for The Minack in the early summer with the particular challenge of using every nook and cranny there.

Kneehigh Theatre start 1990 with another original move. Mike Shepherd has been working with Charles Causley to adapt one of Causley's favourite children's stories, *The Tinderbox,* for the stage. Production should start at Easter but it will be touring the South West in the autumn as the company are off to the Continent again in the summer.

For the future, Kneehigh Theatre plan to retain their Cornish base, to become more involved in education and, in fact, to become a 'resource for Cornwall', their aim being to entertain, tell stories and reflect the state of the times and the planet.

Pauline Sheppard

Martin Val Baker (September 1988)

Incredibly, Shiva Theatre of Penzance complete their first decade of existence this month To celebrate the occasion I talked to Pauline Sheppard. Shiva's administrator/adaptor/actress about the company's precarious career.

Shiva Theatre evolved from performances of two one-act plays at the first St Ives Festival in 1978. Actors David Shaw and Brian Slogget played to packed houses on the festival fringe and were inspired to take the plays, *Krapps Last Tape* and *The Dumb Waiter* on a tour of other Cornish venues. When asked to provide a name for his company for the festival programme, David offered the name of his newly-acquired cat, Shiva.

Always the mainstay of the company David Shaw (a Penzance man) learnt his trade at Bristol Old Vic, Ipswich, Canterbury and finally through a very long run in the West End comedy *No Sex Please We're British.* Finally, bored by the tedium of what had become a regular job, David returned to Penzance, where he opened a record shop and eventually became involved in the local theatre scene.

After the success of their one-act plays Shiva applied to South West Arts for a grant for a further production—"going up to Exeter and doing everything right." SWA came down, liked the one-acts, and granted Shiva £1,000 towards a major show, a source of funding that continued for several years.

For their next production, Shiva chose *Dylan* by Sidney Michaels, covering the poet's last days.

"In those days we thought that a good play that had not been done professionally before in Cornwall could run for a week in each of the Cornish venues—Newquay, St Austell, Falmouth and St Ives. It doesn't work, though! The only play that might have worked like that was Aykbourn's *Bedroom Farce,* which sold out the Guildhall twice at the 1979 St Ives Festival but that had only just been released from the West End."

In the late 'seventies, the great Footsbarn were still in Cornwall and, not wishing to complete with them. Shiva concentrated on the gap for good Rep plays such as *Bedroom Farce, Sleuth Bodies* and *Who's Afraid of Virginia Woolf.* Northcott Theatre had stopped touring and there was a dearth of good live theatre this side of Exeter.

Shiva Theatre lost their SWA grant after doing a highly successful tour with *Play It Again Sam,* by Woody Allen. "It was one of the longest and far-reaching tours we have ever done—full houses nearly everywhere. Everyone seemed to enjoy it, except SWA, whose major criticism was that there was no social, sexual, or political significance which actually shows a great lack of understanding of the comedy of Woody Allen."

I asked Pauline what she thought about the policy of giving one company in each area the majority of the Regional Arts Association's Theatre allocation (in our case to Orchard Theatre) in order to provide one company of excellence. "They couldn't give enough money to achieve excellence. Orchard are now a step up and can do everything properly but, while not knocking their actors, it will always remain small scale rather than the 'company of excellence' that the South West needs."

Shiva Theatre always apply to SWA for a grant when the annual handout time comes round but, "It doesn't help much unless they give you a lot of money. There are far too many strings with a SWA grant."

Shiva's planning policy generally is to put on the more serious plays in the winter and to try and capitalise on the influx of visitors by producing a comedy each summer. Most local people are not aware of the vast distances covered by Shiva during their winter tours outside Cornwall. the company command fixed fees as they market themselves through intensive publicity shots and phone calls.

"This time last year we were in Folkestone. In April we finished the *Three Musketeers* tour, which began in August last year. We went to Liverpool, Manchester, the East Midlands, London, the Isle of Wight..."

When Shiva tour up-country, they have had help from North West Arts, Southern Arts, South East Arts, Mid Pennine Arts and Mid Wales Arts though not recently from South West Arts!

Locally, Carrick Council have been very helpful and Penwith have given a bit. Cornwall County Council have aided Shiva in the past, but a new rule has come in whereby CCC in future will only give grants to companies receiving money from SWA so that source is now dry. The economics of touring, mean that often Shiva travel with four or five-handers, although The *Three Musketeers* involved eight or nine people. On top of everything else, Pauline used to be Shiva's driver, but now the company boasts three people with a licence and David's son, Martin, as lighting technician.

For some years Shiva Theatre did regular Schools productions, but withdrew when Kneehigh Theatre devoted a separate company to the schools. "It wasn't a direct decision, but we became aware that we'd be doing it at the same time and, coincidentally, Michael Dyer asked us to do a Schools Week at The Minack Theatre".

The Minack production was a great success and now Shiva have a two-week show for schools every June. At the Minack, the company works under the over-all title of The Cornwall Theatre Company, or its subsidiary, Shiva Schools Productions, which enables the actors to work with youth groups and occasional outside performers.

Although Shiva Theatre is, for David and Pauline, a full-time occupation, its economics are often unpredictable and quite often they can be seen in TV films and adverts, or performing with Shiva's cabaret outfit, The Jungle Band, to earn a few extra pennies.

A touring company will play one night to ten people, the next to two hundred. What makes the chemistry work? "If they help you with the get-in and give you a cup of tea, then they'll get a good show—it's good psychology. It's the greeting that counts. The north-west venues could not be more helpful—Accrington Town Hall, a disco in Blackburn, a school in Northwich were all atrocious as venues, but the people could not do enough for us They appreciated that we had come a long way. There's no reason why that can't happen elsewhere."

Often Shiva adapt plays over fifty years old (and thus out of copyright) to save on royalties, which can be up to 10 per cent of the gross takings. A more modern project is in the pipeline and, if Pauline's adaptation is approved, will be produced next year.

Meanwhile, Shiva's involvement with the revitalised art centre at Penzance, The Acorn, has come at an opportune moment. After ten years, there is always a danger of 'burn out', but The Acorn has in a sense regenerated the company, especially through the opportunity to work with actors and musicians from other groupings.

It is in Shiva's interests to have as many performers involved in the venture, though the company will always rehearse and open their tours at The Acorn.

As we concluded the interview, an actor wandered by clutching a £50 note—things are looking good for Shiva Theatre!

Mike Silver

Martin Val Baker (April 1989)

In the summer of 1969 a successful live music club, run on much the same lines as today's Acorn, flourished at the Railway Hotel, Penzance. Throughout the season the club featured the best of the local musicians six nights a week, with regular spots for club organiser Goudie Charles' Jazz Roots & Kris Gayle, The Famous Jug Band, The Temple Creatures and a promising young songwriter called Mike Silver. Twenty years on, Mike returned for a gig at The Acorn and afterwards talked to the Voice about his adventures in the music business.

Mike Silver was born in Berkshire, spending his early life on a farm before moving to London with his family when he was ten. An early musical influence was the record collection of his elder brothers, numbers by such 'fifties heroes as Gene Vincent, Lonnie Donnegan and the Chris Barber Jazz Band.

Mike's first musical instrument was a ukulele, though he soon moved to a guitar, bought from the proceeds of a newspaper round. Entirely self-taught, Mike quickly learned enough chords to play 'Shadows stuff' with a friend at local youth club dances. Soon, he was playing rhythm guitar and singing harmony vocals with R&B bands on the South London club circuit. In fact, work was in such a plentiful supply that Mike overdid it a bit and came to the verge of physical and mental exhaustion, eventually rejoining his family, who had by now moved down to Kent, in search of a quieter life.

It was in Kent that Mike Silver first came across a folk club, and, much impressed, he surrendered his electric instrument in favour of an acoustic and made his first attempt at song-writing. In 1969 and 1970 Mike based himself in West Cornwall for the summer season, playing regularly at the Railway Club and also at the Mermaid Club at Gurnard's Head, another haven for good music.

A friend of Mike's, Mike Beason, had written a story for a newspaper competition called *The Applicant*, the sad tale of Mr Beason's search for employment, and the two of them combined to produce a 'folk opera' from it. With the help of American singer Jackson C. Frank, who saw an excerpt, *The Applicant*, with words by Beason and songs by Silver, was released on the Phillips Fontana label and is a classic of its kind, although little effort was put into the promotion of the record.

In 1971, Mike teamed up with former 'Mermaid of Zennor' Chrissie Quayle and American guitarist Steve Hayton to form the band Daylight, recording a promising album with RCA which featured eight of Mike's songs. According to Mike, "they gave us a load of money, and we blew it."

After the demise of Daylight, Mike performed solo for a while as Mike Boreham: "I felt really good about using my name, though it's not a particularly good name for going on stage—in some ways it's a bit sad having a stage name.

At last success beckoned. With the help of record producer Del Newman (who had worked on Cat Steven's early albums), Mike submitted a demo tape of his songs to Elton John's Rocket label. The five directors of Rocket all enthused about the songs and offered Mike a record deal, with the stipulation that he changed his name back from Boreham to Silver. Mike Silver's album *Troubadour*, produced by Del Newman, features some superb songs, including Mike's favourite, Pioneers' Return, a tribute to Bob Dylan, and surely deserved better treatment than it received. The problem seems to have been that Elton himself apparently didn't like the end result and consequently although it was released in America (where Mike was practically unknown), It never saw the light of day in the UK where he had growing band of followers.

Looking back, Mike is still a little bemused by this action and while admitting to one or two faults on the record feels quite confident about its over-all quality. Although a possible spot as a support on Elton's American tour now fell through, Mike was sent off by Rocket to the States on a promotional solo tour of the club circuit—some of which were so grotesquely unsuitable for his music that his self-confidence was shattered.

With the decision not to release *Troubadour* in the UK, Mike's Rocket career came to an end and he went to Holland for a fortnight. The two weeks turned into a seven-year stay, during which he married Dutch singer Christine Etterman and toured extensively through Europe: "Sometimes Christine would be playing Newcastle whilst I would be in Munich." At this time Mike recorded an LP in Germany, *Come and be my Lady*, as well as *Midnight Train* (1979), produced by Jo Partridge for Sarn Records, a record that he feels particularly proud of. Other LPs were to follow: *Silver Songs* recorded in Denmark in 1981; another German record *Let's Talk About You*, in 1983, as well as two albums on his own label, Silversounds, *Free* and the most recent, *There's No Machine* in 1987.

These days, Mike plays mostly in Britain, getting a lot of work in northern folk clubs, though he does not see himself as a folk singer: "If you categorise music you put borders on it and don't give it much of a chance."

Mike is a bit worried about 'Roots' label, too, feeling that 'World Music' is being promoted to such an extent that it might swamp the best of the home-grown variety. However, he can see the beginnings of a revival in the clubs, with new young performers and audiences providing much stimulation—he mentions Lee Colinson as a guitar player to watch.

Rather than organising tours as such, Mike takes bookings as they come although he is wary of geographic implications, not enjoying long journeys as he used to. He is also a little more choosy about doing gigs at unsuitable venues, not needing the money enough to play in an unsympathetic environment. Mike finds being on the road quite an insular existence, "stuck in a car for four hours and then you have to get out and be full of the joys of spring, go on stage and be really happy!" In fact, he has written a song about this very subject, *The Jester*, on the *Troubadour* album.

Recently, Mike has combined forces with his contemporary, Allan Taylor and co-produced an LP, once again seeing the significance of the producer. "It's vital to have someone who can be objective about the music. The producer's job is to draw things out of the artist, rather than to change anything."

Alex Smirnoff

Martin Val Baker (November 1989)

From time to time the somewhat familiar exhibits on the walls of the local galleries are disturbed by an exciting new talent. Narrative painter Alex Smirnoff is a relative newcomer to the area, having arrived just over a couple of years ago, but already his provocative paintings, many based on local folklore, are attracting the red dots at an impressive rate.

Alex was born in London in 1960, although he grew up and was educated in Sussex. From 1977 until 1981 he studied graphic design at the West Sussex College of Design. Soon after leaving college, Alex became disillusioned with graphics and gradually drifted into illustration whilst working at a series of odd jobs in London during the mid-'80s. Never one to push himself, Alex became "much happier as a fine artist, where I do the work and people can come and buy or not buy!" In fact, it is only in the last two years that he has been able to make "almost a living" from his paintings.

For some years before moving to Cornwall, Alex had been spending his holidays in the county, so when he became fed up with the south-east there was only one place to go—he had "always felt at home here." As a student he had discovered the stone circles and ancient monuments of Cornwall and became absorbed by the region's folklore, researching in local libraries and building up a collection of books on the subject. These studies were to inspire a series of paintings based on the folk legends of Cornwall which he started unsuccessfully in Sussex but which eventually came to fruition when he moved to Penwith.

A good example of these is *The Hooting Cairn*, which was suggested by the tale of two miners led astray by the Devil in disguise whilst returning from Morvah, who are only rescued from the clutches of a gang of wrestling demons by the accidental invocation of the name of God.

Alex does not now see himself as an illustrator as he happily strays from the literal path and takes the legends as merely a starting point. Often he will go to a particular location and sit and draw, hoping to be able to put some of the atmosphere into his painting, but many of his best drawings are done from memory away from the location.

All the work at Alex Smirnoff's recent WOLF AT THE DOOR show has been done since Christmas; indeed several were sold paintings 'called in' to make up the numbers. One was a particularly striking double 'portrait in a landscape' that had been commissioned. Many of the paintings have been reproduced in greeting card form, provoking the thought that there would be a good market for larger prints.

At the moment, Alex is finding it difficult to keep up with demand. A number of people think his work is under-priced, but he is happy making a living at what he wants to do and would rather sell a lot perhaps too cheaply than risk over-pricing and not selling so much.

Confessing to being "a bit of a hermit," Alex has not yet got too involved with other local galleries, although he was very pleased with his first show at VISIONS AND JOURNEYS at St Just. Next summer, he plans a solo show at The Ice House, in London's Holland Park, where he had a successful mixed show some years ago: "I've never had to go out and shout; I always seem to stumble across the right people at the right time."

Alex finds it impossible to work on more than one painting at a time and he commits himself to an environment scattered with working drawings and photographs relating to the work in progress.

The thought of a book appeals to him (he has several ideas for story lines), but he is not keen to return to illustrating as such and enjoys the way he works now. "I haven't got the pressures an illustrator has, I do what I want. I don't have to keep strictly to the narrative that I'm taking my inspiration from."

Heroes and influences include Stanley Spencer and early Flemish artists, Van Eyck, Bruegel and Bosch. (One of the paintings on display at the Wolf was very heavily varnished, giving it a quite ancient feel.) He has already completed a couple of triptychs and is keen to follow the path of using several panels to convey a narrative. In a separate but related discipline, he has done several carvings inspired by church bench ends.

Locally, Smirnoff is impressed by the "Ancientness" of Penwith's landscape, with its organic hedges—"even the buildings seem to be growing out of the landscape. And the little subtleties—all the best things about Penwith don't hit you in the eye; you can go down a little wooded valley and you will see all the gnarled trees, lichen and rocks, little details in the landscape that you have to search for."

Sometimes, Alex gets the urge to broaden out: "People say it's okay, but not so good as my normal stuff. I'm aware that my strength is in my more meticulous work—it's that which seems to excite people. I'm constantly tidying up—I'll start a painting thinking I'll keep this one broad, and then I'll tighten up and tighten up because I can't stand a wonky finger or something.

"I hate failure in my work, so if I feel an idea isn't going to work early on it's rejected. I can spend two or three weeks on preparatory drawing and getting things ready for a painting, start it and then give it up, so I've wasted all those weeks. It's really frustrating, putting all that effort into something and then putting it on a wall and realising that it's not right.

"If I feel the idea is fundamentally sound, but I'm having trouble painting it, I won't give up on that—it's the idea that has to be right, no matter how hard the actual painting process is.

"The Sancreed Rood Screen painting in the Wolf show had to be repainted and repainted all the time over a couple of months because I knew that if I could finish it, then it would be all right."

Maurice Sumray

Sue Monro (August 1989)

After twenty years in St Ives, surrounded by stunning views from his house on Porthmeor Beach, the area remains for Maurice Sumray an inspirational desert. He still prefers the buzz of a late-night gambling den in the metropolis to being marooned in a seaside resort listening to "the interminable waffle of the arty crowd."

Yet the move to Cornwall proved fortuitous (possibly more for the connoisseurs of his paintings than for himself) as he had ceased painting in 1953 and, feeling in need of a clean slate, burned all his previous work. He commented, "This was during my conceited phase ... I thought I was the cat's whiskers, that I'd done it all."

Twenty years later, he was persuaded by his wife to fill empty wall spaces with his own work and was amazed to find "all the living and dying" he had managed in the meantime had no effect on style or content. Now in his 69th year, the sable brushes still flow.

Sumray left school at an early age. He confessed, "I wasn't clever enough to win a scholarship. In fact, I was almost expelled for being such a dunce." His father encouraged him to train as an engraver and so successful was this side of his life that he eventually set up his own hand-printed textile business and contributed toward the development of the flexographic printing process.

He spent the war years working in the Ministry of Economic Warfare and fighting fascism as an active member of the Hogarth Group.

Fifteen years were to pass before he resumed his formal education with the aid of a scholarship to London University/Goldsmiths College of Art. The intervening years were far from wasted. In fact, Sumray considers he had done most of his best work before going to Goldsmiths and had little to learn from the tutors: "As excellent as they were in their chosen fields, I had already developed my own style and would rather have been influenced by looking at a Rembrandt." Indeed, by 1950 the accolades were pouring in. Wyndham Lewis described him as "one of the two best artists in England" following his exhibition at Gimpel Fils. More recently, the British Museum purchased two of his works.

While it's virtually impossible to separate the enigmatic jigsaw of Sumray's life and persona from his paintings, influences and obsessions do emerge. He maintains his childhood years were happy and relatively free of financial worries "Mother was firm and good, she always encouraged us. When Father died, she went out to work." Yet the poverty, suffering and appalling living conditions he witnessed in the East End have haunted his visual images and shaped his commitment to society's underdogs ever since.

The despair and isolation of the persecuted ethnic minorities and social outcasts that he concentrated on in his early portraits evoke the emotional intensity of a Goya and the social comment of a Daumier

He admits his later work lost some of this sensitivity; individual emotions were sacrificed to the overall aesthetic effect. His exquisitely crafted clowns, jugglers, acrobats and dancers strive toward perfection in a far from perfect world. Some are subtly charged with erotic innuendo, others pin you down with a penetrating gaze. All are related by similar facial features and they cling together to block out the loneliness that threatens to engulf them. But melancholia never takes over, there are always distractions ... radiating lines from perfectly-positioned ladders, chairs, wings, signboards, explosions of colour from delicate flowers, all arranged to complement the figures and producing an over-all feeling of mirror-like stillness.

Sumray says he has no intrinsic interest in his romantic stage figures: "They just drift out from subconscious inner feelings without my being intellectual about them." And he doesn't recognise the symbolism other people see in his paintings. He puts his obsessional striving toward perfection in every meticulous detail of his work down to the technical discipline that was required of him as an engraver.

Money for money's sake has never been Sumray's prime motive—any surplus tended to end up on a poker table or in his own art collection, which has since been sold to pay bills. He feels that if he had been forced to earn a living out of selling his paintings, he would have pushed himself to produce more. As it is, he spends up to two years on each large canvas. This indicates to him that he should never have been a painter, but it does help to defeat one of his other obsessions, boredom. He admits to not having enjoyed painting since he was 18: "Painting for me is a battle, I find the medium difficult."

He worries about running out of visual images, claims his powers of observation are limited, says he is hopeless at drawing, views life without colour and claims none of his work is finished to his total satisfaction.

Not only is he frequently plagued by self-doubt about his own work, he questions the role of the artist in society. He considers the task of drawing public awareness to social injustice is frequently better achieved by writers rather than painters and that most of the best artists remain unknown while many of the famous ones produce rubbish. He is particularly scathing about the latter-day St Ives School, which he describes as "a myth, lacking in any English tradition—it frequently rides on the crest of American expressionism."

On the other hand, he is not precious about his own work and doesn't mind if his paintings are hung upside down or if he is called a figurative illustrator; he commented, "Whatever I say about other people, the finger can always be pointed at me because I'm as guilty."

The unassuming side of this complex man often escapes those who have been on the receiving end of his more outspoken views. This side has recently taken him into muddy waters with the Newlyn Society of Artists, who requested his resignation after he interrupted a lecture. He didn't agree with the lecturer's assertion that poets knew nothing about painters. An argument ensued. As far as Sumray is concerned "If they want to boost the Society, they should show good art and stop criticising their members." He refuses to resign; the fiasco rumbles on.

Despite the fact that Sumray rarely exhibits, his paintings are in great demand, particularly by the dealers—and not just for their rarity value. As he said, "people either go crazy about my work or they hate it." As with the man there are no half measures.

June Tabor

Martin Val Baker (December 1989)

In the field of British contemporary folk music over the past two decades, there have been four dominant female singers; the late Sandy Denny of Fairport Convention, Maddy Prior of Steeleye Span, Jaqui McShee of Pentangle and the unpredictable June Tabor. Last month, June was in Penzance to give two concerts at The Acorn, made notable by the wide breadth of material chosen. Before leaving for the next gig of a nationwide tour to promote her new jazz flavoured LP *Some Other Time,* she talked to the *Voice.*

June Tabor (her real name) was born and brought up in Warwick, later moving to Oxford where she studied Modern and Medieval History. It was this background that eventually secured her a job as a librarian in North London, a career she was able to continue whilst making her first forays into the folk world. In fact, it comes as a surprise to learn that, in contrast to many of her contemporaries, June has only been 'on the road' full-time for the last couple of years, having later run a restaurant in the north for five years.

As a teenager, June had no formal musical training at all. She always enjoyed singing, but had 'a strange voice that didn't fit in with the expected altos and sopranos at school.' At one time, she attempted to learn whistle and concertina, but gave up gracefully ("I was too lazy to practice") and these days is quite happy to hire musicians to accompany her songs.

Like most of her generation, she was an avid Beatles and Stones fan, later being very impressed by the early Fairports. Soon she was singing with a soft rock band which was "a cross between Fairport and Janis Joplin—we used to finish with *Piece of my Heart."* At the same time, influenced by the singing of Anne Briggs and Belle Stewart, June had started singing traditional songs in the folk clubs and doing short spots at festivals. Soon this developed into a club act of two half-hour spots: "That's about the limit for an unaccompanied singer, however much you vary it through humour, chorus songs and so on." She does feel, though, that the same formula is a bit dangerous in a concert situation.

Gradually, her reputation grew and from 1972 June was invited to make a series of guest recordings culminating in a first album of her own in 1976, *Airs and Graces* with Nic Jones (guitar) and Jon Gillespie (keyboards). The same year also saw the release of the first 'Silly Sisters' record with Maddy Prior, who June had met up with earlier whilst still at Oxford: "We were singing together in the back row, singing harmonies at a festival, and Maddy said, 'that sounds nice, why don't we try and work out something together?'."

In 1977, June toured to promote her new record, *Ashes and Diamonds.* As Nic Jones was not available, she teamed up with guitarist Martin Simpson, an alliance that was to last ten years, including a performance at the St Ives Festival of 1979. The Tabor/Simpson combination was a fine pairing offering the variants of June (solo), June and Martin, Martin as guitarist, Martin as banjo-player, and included a strong grouping of American Civil War songs. June has always felt, as a non-instrumentalist, that the words of a song are vitally important, and she goes to some trouble to find good lyrics: "You can turn a mediocre tune into something better than it really is, but you can't do anything with a mediocre set of words."

Two more LPs were released, *A Cut Above* (1980) and *Abyssinians* (1983) before her five-year stint as a restaurateur: "Never again!" During this time, she kept her hand in with occasional gigs and recording sessions, including one for John Peel.

In 1988 the restaurant was sold and June moved to north Cumbria, where her neighbours include Maddy Prior, Rick Kemp and Michael Chapman, all of whom are not averse to the odd local pub gig!

At the suggestion of an American record label, Maddy and June recorded another 'Silly Sisters' album and the same year June's acclaimed *Aqaba* was released. By now, Martin Simpson had left for America and June asked keyboard player Huw Warren (who had impressed her on the 'Silly Sisters' session) to join her as accompanist. Both Huw and sax player Mark Lockheart come from a classical and jazz background: "They have had nothing to do with folk music, which is great for me—an entirely different influence is brought in on arrangements and choice of materials and working with keyboards opens up a whole new field of material not available to voice and guitar. Martin Simpson is unique; another guitar player would have invited comparisons. It's right to do something entirely different—you must keep changing for your own head!"

Recently, June has become an admirer of the 'Songsearch' songwriting competition. She was a judge one year and from the finalists she introduced two of the songs into her repertoire. The following year, though not a judge, she asked to hear a tape of the finalists and picked out *Where are you Tonight?* which also appeared on *Aqaba.* "These contests are well worth doing for someone like me. It's remarkable what comes out, even without a large financial prize."

Another song on *Aqaba* was given to her in Los Angeles by its author, Natalie Merchant of 10,000 Maniacs who, it turned out, was something of a fan of June's. Yet another song, the title track, was commissioned from Bill Caddick.

She and Huw have just returned from a six-week tour of the States. The present tour is to promote the new LP, a collection of jazz standards which also features Danny Thompson and Bosco D'Olivera. It's a record that grew out of the successful introduction of some jazz numbers into June's mainly folk set. She sees this as a sideways move rather than any major change in direction and is aware that it frightened some of her listeners. However, she says, "Listen to the words; they all tell a good story and that's what traditional music is all about"

She would love to work with a big band but sees that as impossible financially, though she is quite happy working with Huw: "I flap a lot and he doesn't flap at all. I still get terribly nervous, usually over PAs because they show up so much in what I do."

The setting and atmosphere is important to June and she is very conscious of where her performance will or will not work: "You can suddenly find yourself working to a bar audience where neither they nor the artist can concentrate. I have to make sure that promoters realise that we must help the audience concentrate, because what I do is very intense and it requires intense concentration. It's based on the words and you've got to hear them to understand the performance. I need help in that sense, and so does the audience."

Like many modern performers, June enjoys working with different combinations of musicians. She has just done a song for Les Barker's new folk opera *The Stones of Callanish.*

Another interesting venture involves working with Mark Emerson of Pyewakett with voice and violin, or voice and viola, using the voice as instrument as well as for singing. June and Huw have also arranged some of their material for string, sextet (two violins, two violas, two cellos) and gave a concert at the London Purcell Rooms: "And it worked, I'd love to do more of that."

RSC

Betty Thatcher

Martin Val Baker (March 1988)

Betty Thatcher has lived in Cornwall for over twenty years and in that time she has moved from St Ives to Hayle and from working as a dishwasher to becoming a successful songwriter. In the 'seventies she wrote lyrics for such top bands as *Renaissance, Vinegar Joe, Supertramp* and *Racing Car* amongst others, and more recently she has co-written a musical which should be staged in the West End in the next couple of years.

Although very much a Londoner (she was born near Oxford Circus), she was once described in *Melody Maker* as "the Cornish Poet Betty Thatcher" and I asked her how that came about.

"Oh that was the *Renaissance* manager, it was a really good publicity stunt, and it worked, it got people interested but everyone thought I was about ninety!"

Betty arrived in St Ives as a teenage café worker in the early 'sixties and like so many city refugees of that time was captivated. She was soon involved with that strange community of ex-patriates who worked hard through the summer and lived on porridge through the tough winters. One summer Betty became friendly with another Londoner, Jane Relf, and when Jane returned home wrote a letter with impressions of St Ives life. Jane showed the letter to her brother, the rock musician Keith Relf of *The Yardbirds,* who was immediately impressed and asked her if she would be interested in writing some songs.

"I didn't know who he was, but he said that he and the drummer Jim McCarty would write the music if I did the words and gave me £1,000 in advance! It was the only time I have ever been rich and he told me not to spend it on anything else but a house—which I did!"

At that time Keith was becoming increasingly bored with his 1960s Blues group *The Yardbirds* and was interested in starting a band combining classical and rock styles, it was for this band, *Renaissance,* that Betty began her career as a professional lyricist. The band's first singer was Jane Relf but very soon she was lured into the world of TV commercials to be replaced by Annie Haslam (who, incidentally, came from Fowey). Over the next few years *Renaissance* became huge in the USA. with a large and dedicated following, with Betty now doing most of the lyrics and Micky Dunford writing the music.

Lyricist and composer share their royalties 50/50 and, in fact, get as much and sometimes more than the performer. Most people would imagine that as a fairly successful songwriter (Betty has had nine albums in the American charts) she must have done well economically —but not so! Betty had to sue for unpaid royalties and. although she won the six year court case, in the end there was no money in the kitty to pay her with. "I worked for all those years and got nothing, I'm not at all unusual, I'm just an ordinary songwriter, but now I have a solicitor to protect me, I get the money up-front."

On several occasions Betty went to the USA with *Renaissance* but found the glamour difficult to cope with. At one time her song *Mother Russia,* written after reading *One Day in the Life of Ivan Denisovitch,* became extremely popular and Betty had to introduce it on stage to an audience of 5,000 at an Amnesty concert. "Suddenly they all lit matches and started chanting my name, I froze with horror, I hated it, I thought, God if they think I'm special the world's just going to fall apart and I fled the stage in terror." Not then, a frustrated performer!

Betty is obviously a little bemused by the American rock world, even getting a friend to sign albums as 'Betty Thatcher' though she is touched by the perseverance of one English fan, Keith Took; "His whole life revolves around visiting rock and film stars at their homes, day and night. They usually cook for him. He writes me long letters at Christmas telling me what he's done and who he's met."

In 1979, *Renaissance* changed musical direction (aiming for the *Genesis* market) and Betty cut her connection with the band—which split up soon after. For the next four years Betty worked as a lyricist with the rock arranger Louis Clark, who was closely involved with *Queen* and *ELO.*

Eventually, however, Clark became a millionaire for his arrangements of the *Hooked on Classics* series, although he did work with Betty again on the single and LP *Still Life,* on which Betty put words to some well-known classical themes. *Still Life* is due for release in America this year but, as it would be uneconomic to tour with the artists who made the album (The Royal Philharmonic Orchestra, Royal Choral Society and Annie Haslam), promotion might prove a little difficult!

A couple of years ago, Betty's erstwhile writing partner, Micky Dunford, approached her to write a musical based on the story of *Scheherazade (A Thousand and One Nights),* a version of which had been recorded live by *Renaissance* at Carnegie Hall. At first, Betty was apprehensive of re-treading old ground but, as work was a bit quiet at the time, she decided to have a go and with the help of an Enterprise Allowance grant spent a year on the project. Both Betty and Micky thought it important to keep artistic control over their work and have resisted the temptation to sell their interests to other producers. They have raised the backing (£2m) to put the show on "but there's still no money in it for us." However, if the musical is a success and it fills an average theatre, Betty and her partner could earn as much as £4,000 a week each. Freddie Mercury of *Queen* has been approached to do an album of the show's music (which includes several possible singles) and other well-known rock stars are lined up to perform the main role when the show goes on.

Betty still, however, prefers the band and recording side of the business to the world of the theatre and still works with bands—she has written several songs for local singer Wendy Herman of *The Bad Boys.* Recently, an old contact rang up from the States offering her the chance to work with a promising band of eighteen-year-olds who have already won a Grammy award for their first album. A challenge that Betty looks forward to with delight. At least this project looks more promising than the time when she was hired to put English words to a number of Spanish pop tunes. "It was very difficult, horrible—some of those tunes were really revolting!" she remembers.

If things did go wrong and she did end up washing dishes again she wouldn't really mind. "It doesn't really matter—it would be a lot easier." One thing is certain—she will be a lot more careful with the earnings. "I was an idiot, I trusted everybody. You can only trust a solicitor and even then you have to be careful."

It must be a great burden to be lumbered with such an unfortunately emotive name as Thatcher and Betty has taken the ultimate step of rejection by changing her surname by Deed Poll. From now on, she reverts back to her original name, Newsinger (yes really!). "I just don't want to give that woman any more publicity, I hate her."

D.M. Thomas

David Scott (March 1991)

The novels of D.M. Thomas, better known than his also considerable output of poems, have been notable for arousing controversy amongst both public and critics. A film of *The White Hotel*, under the directorship of David Lynch and now approaching production will certainly widen the audience for his idiosyncratic blend of myth, history, politics and love in the holocaust.

It's pure coincidence that Cornwall are playing Berkshire on the galeblown afternoon we drive to Truro to interview the author, finally pushing down a narrow sunken drive ('vaginal') to the converted coach house and the circle of garden ('womb like'). A friendly welcome, an impressively stocked library, a three-legged cat, some quick and intensive outdoor photography and we are introduced.

On the study wall is a diagram of a Colombian silver mine in which his uncle once worked: "It's a symbol. I feel there's a parallel between mining and writing. You've got to get all the workable ore from a mine before you close it down."

Then rearrange decently the skirts of the earth, as the Indians used to do?
Myth is important to me and its relationship to history.

And the relations between artists and society?
You must be thinking of *The Flute Player*—that's one of the bases of that novel.

Was the snakes and ladders structure of the background intentional—preconceived?
Very much so. What isn't so preconceived is the path of a character within. You know roughly where characters are sailing to, but how they get there may be obscure until the overall plot unfolds to give a route for them.

You spent two years without writing. Did the urge depart or were you just unable to get it down?
I'm an obsessive writer but for that time nothing surfaced, nothing appealed enough to say 'Write me'. Then I started the memoir, something I needed to do before going on again.

The relationship between the poet and the muse is another persistent theme. Do you see a relationship between Eros and creative writing?
They're hard to disentangle—there's a common impulse In fact, the last weekend course here was on erotic writing. We had six women and one man, but it went very well and they produced some excellent writing out of it.

Do you find it a solitary process, writing?
Well, it is. There's something almost secretive about it. I think it should be essentially subversive; it starts off as a mistress with that flavour of forbidden fruit. Later, of course, it becomes a wife with whose vagaries you have to learn to live.

I notice an absence of short stories in your output.
It's never appealed as a form. I've always dealt with shorter themes by poetry and bigger ones as novels. It's for a different type of writer but, so far, not for me.

Also a certain sparsity of description.
Well, I'm not good at it. I leave it to whom it comes naturally and concentrate on the areas of human and political relations, which is more where my interest lies. Writing's like any other craft—you hide your weaknesses and capitalise on your strengths.

What brought you back to Cornwall?
The circumstances were partly economic. When the college in Hereford looked like being axed, I threw myself into the campaign to save it—posters, pamphlets, petitions and so on. I liked that—working as part of a team with a worthy end in view. Anyway, we failed and as my friends and colleagues drifted elsewhere, I became tired of the area. I'd never really settled there; the earth was too red, the landscape too soft. I wanted granite and moor, the cliffs and the sea. As well as that, I'd done all the writing about Cornwall I could from outside. The mine was worked out and I needed to sink a new shaft to see it again. There's a balance down here. I always think of the moors and headlands, the sea, as being the male part, the wooded estuaries as a female part of the landscape. For all that, we nearly pulled out of settling. The day we arrived to take possession I was on the phone to Hereford in a panic to see if the place there had been sold. It was November and the green cover that enhanced the summer charms of this house was all blown away.

You regret it?
I wouldn't say so, but I like the proximity of the station, the possibility of escape.

Here we break for coffee and the end of the match. (Cornwall are fourteen points up as time is called.) Don shares the Cornish enthusiasm for the game, knows the players by name and reputation. The afternoon closes in, the garden elm rocks in the unabated gale. We try to take up but have lost the thread.

The film (of White Hotel)?
Dennis Potter is doing the screenwriting.

You co-operate?
Well, I look at what he's done and we talk. So far, I'm happy with it.

And if they make a hash of it?
You have to let go, which I did when the novel went for publication. You miss it at first, like losing a baby. There's a Russian word 'Toska'—the Welsh word is 'Hereth'—but there's no exact equivalent in English for 'a bitter sweet melancholy'.

The Russian quartet—something almost predictive there?
I'm not a cause writer. I don't address myself directly to political issues in the same way as I don't feel obliged to write about Cornwall. I might and probably will, but it depends on the muse [said with an expressive shrug].

[A clatter in the kitchen disturbs our flow. One last question]
Influences ?
The family, to some large extent. That unconsciously-structured Cornish speech that's poetry in its own right. There's a poem in that book you have in your hand.

This is 'Perry' whose ... 'hands folded guarded the pear shaped growth she would not have cut out, prodding the flame/stranger, holier than art so set to take possession of her death before it came.'

Then the Russians. Pushkin and Akhomata [who he had translated]. Robert Frost I greatly admire—and a less well-known American poet, Anne Sexton. Causley, of course, but more as a friend and a parallel. Then Jack Clemmo—again, not an influence, particularly, but it's good to see his work existing. And what about John Harris, who deep underground scratched verse in slate with a nail or wrote on discarded tea labels using blackberry juice as the ink his family could not afford? A natural poet.

It's time to pack up. "I've enjoyed it." "And so have we." A courteously-signed copy of the memoir, an invitation to a party "should there be one going on." In the leaking Renault home, a line comes on the wind: 'A fragile myth, a social and a solitary man.'

Kathryn Tickell

Carole Bishop (October 1990)

Kathryn grew up in an extended musical family centred around the village of Wark in the North Tyne Valley. As a child, she learned piano and fiddle and took up the pipes at the age of ten. An early influence was Billy Pigg, the late Northumbrian pipe player. Now, at 23, with three albums behind her, she has toured all over the world, featured in a TV documentary and been voted top instrumentalist in a folk roots poll.

I talked to Kathryn at The Acorn and the following is a transcript of some of her answers to my questions. A prize for the reader who can work out what the questions were.

Roots and Traditions

When I first started playing I wasn't aware that the music was traditional or folk music. My family's one of the few in which music is still very much a way of life. It doesn't happen very often, just in parts of Ireland, Scotland, the Shetland Islands and luckily still in Northumberland.

Going to folk clubs for me was a bit of a culture shock. Before I had the band, while I was still playing solo Northumbrian pipes, I was hailed as some kind of heroine of traditional music. They're not so keen on me now I've got an electric bass in the band!

There's a big difference between traditional music and folk music I can't quite explain what it is but I know It's there. In some folk clubs, there's a lot of importance attached to the age of the tune you're playing and whether you learned it from a shepherd in Northumberland or from somebody who worked in an office in Newcastle

That's being compounded by collectors. I was at a festival in Scotland a few years back and somebody had found this woman of about 80 who sang traditional songs. Before she went on stage this collector who had found her said, "Now what are you going to sing?" and she said, "I'm going to sing this, this and this,"—all the songs she liked, some country songs, some like *The Old Rugged Cross,* anything. He said, "No, don't sing that, don't sing that one, sing that one." In a way it's good because he was picking out songs people hadn't heard, but in another way it presents a totally false image of that woman and her tradition to the public they think she only sings those kind of songs.

I know people have the idea that in the village pub at home everyone plays this wonderful traditional music. If they went in, they'd probably be really disappointed because most of the time there's no music. Sometimes they get the woman from the garage playing her accordion and she'll do *Daisy, Daisy* and war songs, or lads from the football team might get drunk and sing the *Bladen Races.*

Interspersed with that, and on an equal footing, is a traditional song of that particular village or valley, but there's no difference between them. It makes going to the folk clubs a bit strange sometimes

The original type of festivals at home were the shepherds' shows, like Bellingham Show. They often have piping competitions—to pipers they're quite prestigious. Then other festivals started in the towns, in Newcastle, Rothbury and Morpeth They're music festivals, but very different to English festivals. No-one knows who's going to be on but they're always sold out. It's not particularly a folk audience, they're really for the people from the towns.

About a fortnight before my A-levels, it dawned on me for the first time that going professional was a possibility, and I'd been accepted for a place at University. I decided there and then to give it a try for three years, and that was five years ago.

They used to say I was terribly young; every time I got a review it went on that I was 16 or 18. For a long time there weren't any young people playing Northumbrian pipes, but over the last four or five years there's been such a lot of good young musicians it's just brilliant. Lynn, for example, she's just turned 17. So now I'm not getting that tag any more.

It's made such a difference working with the band. Now, going away with them is just great, whereas solo work meant sitting around all day.

This year I've worked in Paris, Finland, Yugoslavia, Canada, France again and Spain Sometimes it's great but when we went to Spain, for example, I got there at six o'clock, played at half past eight for 15 minutes, got up really early the next morning and went straight to the airport and that was it. I might as well have been in Croydon or somewhere.

I'm very pleased with the way this band's going and I do feel that some of the arrangements we're doing are very different and unusual.

I'd love to work with percussion—it's just money at the moment. We've just got established and we would only want a percussionist on half the material. I really like tablas—I've worked with a lot of Asian musicians in Newcastle.

The other thing I'd really love is another fiddle player The sound man, Hudson, he's a really good fiddle player; it's just not very feasible to have him doing the sound and on stage playing, but we're working on It.

The accordion has turned out to be an amazing instrument to have in a band because it can do so many things—harmony, tune, rhythm, bass. It's been quite exciting working with it.

It never occurred to me when I put the band together to get a singer as I had been playing solo for so long and don't sing myself. There are more instrumental bands coming up now, actually. I was playing in a folk club once and had a cold at the time. At the end of the night the MC said, "And wasn't she wonderful! But what's she going to be like when her throat's better and she can sing again!"

I'm sometimes asked to write commissions—I had to write a tune for the 600th anniversary of the Battle of Otterburne. That was one that I wanted to do because my family's from the Borders and I'd heard my dad sing Border ballads. I knew so much about it, I'd heard it all my life. It was good for me to do a tune about that.

Tracks from my records have been used as background music for TV programmes, but I wish they'd ring me up and ask me to do something as it would be much better if I could see something and write music for it. I'd like to be able to do more stuff like that.

I was left with the certain feeling that it's only a question of time before Kathryn is commissioned to compose music for TV and films. Meanwhile, her latest album is 'Common Ground' (Black Crow Records). She can also be heard accompanying Sting on his latest album due to be released soon.

Rod Walker

Ashley Peters (December 1985)

Colour, colour and colour, zappy, zingling colours. Blue heads screaming from yellow backgrounds, a strident chequered black and white dress, a grimacing pink-eyed green man and purple-pink shadows, all in strong designs. These elements appear in Rod Walker's recent work of the theatre world. There are visual puns in these pictures too, glasses which you cannot see through, a microphone and it's lead becomes a snake, a drummer who becomes a snake charmer. A lot of this work has a slightly decadent feel to it. Nightlife.

The theatre is a rich visual vein of humans in an unreal situation. Rod Walker likes the experience of being transported into another reality where things appear to look OK, but not quite right. This fantasy world is his vehicle to express feelings of unease, of being uncomfortable. His surprising choice of bold and vivid colours furthers that experience.

We sit down for the interview in near freezing conditions, gloves, woollies and lots of tea. The stove isn't working yet, surrounded by his big blues, wadges of yellow, bright primary reds, greens and purples. He was brought up in London and attended Epsom Art College. He moved to Cornwall in 1971 and this led to a new sense of freedom which let him loose on colour. Early work was abstract, moving to vibrant and figurative wild animal designs, exotica. There was then a graphic period after a visit to New York in 1982—images of Manhattan skyline, street scenes and a series on the statue of Liberty.

A studio should be an explosion of all sorts of objects, and Rod's is filling up with all manner of things which he has painted. Alongside his highly personal oil painting, he involves himself in the decorative side of the arts for an everyday market. There are painted anecdotes like a saw stuck half-way in a piece of wood. Furniture, books, lamps, jewellery, etc., are all painted up with an element of surprising bright colour, no object s seen as sacred.

In the last twelve months, the abstract properties which he has learnt over the years have come together in his new figurative work of the theatre. His pictures are filling up with more of the world—people, drums, hats, glasses, real curtains draped around a painting and so on. This is important because for him abstract painting can realise it's full potential in figurative painting.

His works can be bought from his studio at 9 St. Philip Street, by appointment with the artist.

Note—Rod Walker feels we owe a cultural debt to Africa. In July 1984 he just finished a painting entitled "Africa" and at this same time he read a *Guardian* report on starvation in Ethiopia. This in turn led him to being an innovator in gathering artists from all over Cornwall to contribute their work freely to an art auction to raise money for Ethiopia. £4,000 was raised and this was before Band Aid, etc.

Roy Walker

Roy Walker (November 1987)

At fifteen I started at Gravesend School of Art in Kent, my home county but wasn't a very good student, rebellious and argumentative. However, they were exciting times for me and it was at this time I became aware of the artist Cezanne and thought he was a god—and still do. Also, when I inadvertently picked up an American Forces programme of Jazz whilst fiddling with the family wireless, I found my hero, Charlie Parker, the Be-Bop jazz alto sax player.

Three years later I was sucked into the R.A.F. to do my National Service with many other eighteen-year-old victims. It was a bumpy period for me, but after the trauma of 'squarebashing', I managed to settle down and paint fairly consistently, in spite of the hostile environment. During this period, Charlie Parker died, and I still remember the deep sense of loss and waste I felt.

On being demobbed I did a celebratory hitch-hike to the South of France and actually stood in Cezanne's studio which looked to me as though he had just popped out for a pee ...

It was really quite untidy and everywhere were objects that I was completely familiar with from his painting. Anyway, I was hooked; the life of art beckoned but it took a lot longer to get it together than I thought then.

Back home, I got a job and enrolled at the Central School of Art in London part-time, doing stained glass, life-drawing, painting, all that kind of thing—but not really making a lot of headway.

In the early part of the 'sixties I married and at about this time started visiting St Ives. By 1966 I was convinced that it was the only place I could work in fruitfully, so I moved down in 1967. However, the first couple of years were completely fruitless as far as painting was concerned; nothing seemed to work. Then I was deluged with an outpouring of images that were a shock to me. They were of factory workers and factory-scapes and were the result of probably the worst period of my life which were the three years just before moving to St Ives when I was a production worker on the 'line' at Ford's in Dagenham. It had been such an awful experience that it was the last thing I wanted to see again; they looked so strange in my new environment. However, it was obvious that I was going to have to work through it, so I tentatively started to submit some to the Penwith as an associate member. Some of them were accepted, but I must say they looked very incongruous on the walls

Towards the end of the period that I was working through this factory stuff, which was some kind of exorcism I suppose, things started to happen. Firstly, in 1971, I gave up my full-time job in St Ives to paint full-time instead, a decision my wife supported me in. In the following year I was allocated a Porthmeor Studio which was a tremendous boost for me; at last I had my own space, that dream in Cezanne's studio was a reality.

It wasn't without its fears though; I really thought that with all this extra time, I would run out of ideas but it didn't turn out like that.

I was exhibiting a lot more and in 1973 was elected a full Member of the Penwith Society of Arts.

Some of the other milestones for me in that period were a three-man show at the Marlborough Gallery in London, the Victoria and Albert Museum buying some of my prints and the BBC making a half-hour film about a year in my life which was screened on the television in 1975—so things were beginning to happen. I was also getting more active in the Penwith; running the Print Workshop and towards the end of the 'seventies joined the Committee. In 1979, I was elected chairman of the Society.

In the year following I was invited to have a one-man show in the USA and spent eight weeks there; five of them in Manhattan, which I thought was great.

During the 'eighties I have continued to discover my own particular mode of expression. The art has become much freer and saturated with colour. I work intuitively, allowing my hand to resurrect distilled memories of things seen—silly machines, rusting farm implements, birds, seas, suns and moons and probably some bits of that disgusting factory, trying to get them to co-habit the same space.

I have introduced all kinds of bits and pieces into the work, old envelopes, paper scraps, almost anything that has been discarded, perhaps to precipitate new revelations and transcend their uselessness.

Also during this period I have taken up the challenge of large wall-hanging constructions, working in much the same way I have just described. I just hope that I can continue to tap this, for me, rich vein for the foreseeable future . . .

Hank Wangford

Mike Venning (December 1986)

The audience at Demelza's is laughing, the band is laughing and the singer is delivering his words with a lop-sided grin, but what are they all laughing at? Maybe we'll leave the answer for a while and tune into the memory.

So what was going on? The Hank Wangford Band presented a set of well-played Country and Western to an audience predominantly in its thirties, and I guess you could give .them a bit of discernment. Question .time again: are these people country fans? Picture it—"Hey that dub reggae's a bit passé now, let's give the Louvin Brothers a blast!" or "What about some Bill Monroe tonight?" Well, is that your trendy 'eighties? But there we were, soaking up stuff like "I Ain't Married But The Wife Is" and "Never Wear Mascara When You Love A Married Man", atavistic stuff, or is it?

Hank Wangford likes country music. After a fairly active 'sixties as Sam Hutt, involved in such things as "Frendz" magazine and the making of one of the most obscure and amazing psychedelic singles, "Jabberwocky/Which Dreamed It" by Boeing Duveene and the Beautiful Soup, he took to playing solo C&W in the 'seventies. On the discovery of the Hank Wangford side of his personality, he formed the mark one Wangford Band of which he is the only survivor. The present line-up has been working together for a couple of years and gigging steadily while also doing some T.V. and "Chaps", a country musical. After Christmas, they'll be appearing on Channel 4 on Sunday nights as Hank presents "The A to Z of C&W" which should be a fascinating series with live music, interviews with country stars and archive footage.

As Hank states, he doesn't laugh at Country Music itself, he laughs at the presentation. What gets him is the absurd, hyperbolic sincerity and the Hi Y'all hamming that seems an essential ingredient of C&W. But then he recognises the problem that country carries on its back and which the nonsense seeks to disguise. Us whites can happily listen to Reggae, Blues or any music of a downtrodden ethnic minority and give our good liberal sympathies to sad stories of oppression, but self-pitying white music, that's for truckers and rednecks isn't it? Country's burden is that it's the music of losers and that's not something to acknowledge, least of all in the States. As Hunter Thompson gets Richard Nixon to say: "You show me a good loser—and I'll show you a loser." Thus C&W threads its way through the more shadowy areas of the Caucasian psyche.

Nevertheless, it's great music and Hank plays it because he enjoys it, and on stage he communicates that enjoyment with ease. He knows his C&W and is selective about his repertoire. The so-called "outlaw" country singers and their ensuing trends don't feature; he's not out to carve some alternative niche for himself. He's a great comedian and adds irony to the proceedings by being left-wing (it's in the blood talking to a couple of politicos who didn't know Hank Wangford from a hole in the ground, I was amazed at the exclamations and reverence when the name Allen Hutt was mentioned). He supports Red Wedge and has worked with Billy Bragg, feeling that however little rubs off on the audience, it's a step in the right direction.

Oh, the unanswered question in the first paragraph—I've got the feeling that Hank Wangford stands up there on stage and gets us to laugh at ourselves—most sincerely.

Conway
Twitty

Jason Wason

Sue Monro (June 1983)

Tall, majestic vases standing side by side, all different shapes and sizes, some with bright red and green tassles hanging from delicate. handles, some with copper pins glowing against a matt black glaze, large ceremonial plates with a timelessness bedded into white glazes ... collectively awe-inspiring and individually unique ... all part of the deceptive simplicity that comes from uncluttered lines, perfect symmetry and Jason's inspired craftsmanship.

Jason was born in Liverpool in 1946. After travelling extensively throughout the Middle East, North Africa and India, he set up a crafts co-operative in Scotland where he continued to work from 1972-76. He then moved to Cornwall and joined the Leach pottery, working under the guidance of Janet and Bernard Leach. Last year he decided to set up his own workshop in a converted engine house near Pendeen, not far from where he lives with his wife and two sons. He has exhibited widely, with work in public and private collections throughout Britain, Japan, U.S.A. and West Germany. He is presently exhibiting in a North West Arts sponsored travelling show. Like many potters, Jason has refined and experimented with traditional techniques, glazes etc. as a means of discovering, developing and extending his own individual style ... "I tend not to bother too much with orthodox glazes, partly because this necessitates a biscuit firing, which in these days of limited energy resources seems overtly wasteful and partly because the biscuit firing itself is somewhat tedious and predictable. I have therefore developed a 'once-fire' technique. Using a wide flat brush, I apply a carefully balanced mixture of mineral oxides when the pots are almost dry, and then I take them up to 1280°C. in one firing. Consequently there is a feeling of immediacy and directness which I prefer. The mixture of oxides produces a black glaze which can be smooth and flat as on the Greek Attic vases, or it can have an almost metallic quality similar to that of black iron. Because orthodox glazes have to be applied quite thickly, they tend to soften and dull the sharply defined profile of a pot, whereas a thin layer of oxide does not ... and so when fired, a change of line will remain as hard-edged as I wish and it often furthers the metallic quality of a pot. Exploration in this field has made me aware of the astonishing number of tones and textures of black that exist ... the Eskimos have twenty-seven words for white!" Jason described the six years he spent at the Leach Pottery as an invaluable time for mastering techniques and acquiring workshop discipline, yet the 'Leach' influence is barely perceptible in his recent work ... only the pure simple lines and occasional glazing technique survive. His pottery is primarily sculptural rather than utilitarian.

The years Jason spent travelling and studying the pottery of prehistoric times has left a profound influence on his work. To a certain extent this associates him with the craftsmen of ancient civilisations ... yet in no way are these inspirational sources so obvious that they become a derivative art form or a collectors' substitute for the real thing, he is by no means a slave to an alien tradition. For he brings his own creative vitality, and search for self-awareness, and in doing so provides a unique combination and arrangement of symbols that does justice to both ancient and contemporary worlds. To quote his own words on the subject: "It is difficult to define my source of inspiration; in the travelling of my early years I absorbed much from other cultures and my soul has become a sort of melting pot for these influences. This is now finding an outlet in my work. I am also very moved by some of the pots of prehistory: Mesopotamia, Sumeria etc. The work of the ancients is more than difficult to equal. One can look back as far as the first agrarian cultures that sprang up in the Tigris-Euphrates Valley around 4000 BC to find exquisite pots, fired in the open with only a few simple oxides for decoration that far surpass many modern pots for sheer vitality and strength of design."

On browsing around Jason's workshop I was struck by the virtual absence of modern pottery gadgets, yet I was surrounded by pots with an intensity and precision that many people mistakenly associate with the highly mechanised workshop. He feels that "present-day potters have become accustomed to the technological aids that flood the market ... push button kilns, instant glazes ... Technology itself has become a God, reliance upon which can invoke its bedfellow 'sloth'. It is a tool which must be handled with great care. Seemingly beneficial at the outset, it has the habit of imposing its grandiose will on ours and we find ourselves following meekly behind. The art schools of today house a host of technological wizardry available to the student, yet too great a variety of options can and often does stifle the imagination, the fostering of which is the key to creativity. "MUCH CAN BE DONE WITH LITTLE". Jason's pottery is in itself both re-affirmation and celebration of this. Excellence of craftsmanship combine with ancient rhythms, ritual and symbolic meaning to produce a powerful yet beautifully balanced statement of man's ability to turn the clay from the Earth into objects fit for the Gods.

John Wells

Mike Venning (September 1987)

1928 proved to be a significant year for John Wells, then a medical student, for he found himself studying painting and drawing under Stanhope Forbes at Anchor Studio, Newlyn, the very studio that he bought nearly twenty years later, and which he still retains today.

Around the same time, while holidaying near Falmouth, he was introduced to some artist friends of a relative, the Nicholsons. Such is the seemingly casual way that important events occur in life, for here were many pointers to the direction John Wells would later take.

A practical man, John continued with medicine, and returned to Cornwall as a doctor on the Scilly Isles. He hadn't neglected art though, and was experimenting and building towards an ultimate aim in many ways. During this time he was in contact with artists such as Ben Nicholson, Naum Gabo and Barbara Hepworth, all of whom were working in the area of art in which his own sympathies lay. The relative isolation of life on the Scillies also gave him time to think, and time to save enough money to allow him a shot at painting full-time. Ever-realistic, John gave himself five years to make or break. He made it, and is still pursuing his singular, strong path in this, his eightieth year.

John Wells is an abstract artist; his minutely considered paintings are distillations of the essence of their original visual stimuli. Pared down to the bare bones, they are not dry, nor are they mere patterns. John has always been a keen observer of his environment, as evinced by his detailed knowledge and love of the cliffs and coastal flora and fauna of West Cornwall. It is interesting to note that he shared this interest with Peter Lanyon, and the two of them walked the coastline together, observing and sketching. The resulting paintings show the contrasting methods of the two men: Lanyon working directly from his drawings, Wells pondering over what had seen and what he had drawn, then painting at a distant remove from his initial studies.

Out of such piercing observation as that of John Wells come the kind of connections that a cursory glance would never reveal. The bare, geometric shapes of his paintings relate with surprising directness to what he has seen, to what is there. He is fascinated by the way a fulmar arcs effortlessly across the face of a cliff, or in the golden section, available naturally in the shape of a snail shell. Coupled with this strength of vision, John applies a remarkable depth of thought and feeling to his work, bringing out resonances and previously undetected layers of meaning—"...Heard melodies are sweet, but those unheard are sweeter."

Although a self-contained artist who continues to follow his own direction through the maze of art trends and fashions, John has been a central figure in the art scene down here, both in Newlyn and St Ives. He is not particularly bothered about exhibiting his work but knows what's going on, and is known and admired in turn by the artistic community. He has two studios now, both of which originally belonged to Stanhope Forbes, and is proud and happy with this oasis of calm in the middle of busy Newlyn. This is not to say he doesn't like the town, it's been his home for forty years, and he knows it intimately. This complex and methodical man has combined in his life the seemingly disparate occupations of artist and doctor, all in an unassuming way. John Wells is a thinker, just as he considers his paintings long and hard until he feels that they're right, so he seems to work at life. He sounds as if that hasn't turned out too badly either: quite an achievement.

Jerry White

Pam Otto (September 1988)

Jerry White is an artist living and working in Penzance who is to have his first one-man show at Wolf at the Door from 12th September to 4th October.

He was born in Crawley in 1952, but later moved with his parents to Guildford, Surrey, where he went to school.

He is a shy and reflective young man with a wry, sardonic sense of humour apparent in all his paintings. After an unhappy and unproductive school life, he turned to painting because, as he says, there wasn't anything else left.

He went first to Loughborough, where he was encouraged to develop his ideas and to discover his personal creative idiom. It would seem that his basic education shapes his work even to this day. His work is intensely individual and personal, reminiscent in style of the Glaswegian artists, Ian MacCullouch and Jock McFadyen.

After Loughborough, he went on to the Royal Academy, London; a very different kettle of fish, where everything appeared dry and over-academic: "full of statues and dust." Where once there had been openness there was oppression and a closing of doors. However, one has the distinct impression that Jerry, although quiet, has a streak of stubbornness which has enabled him to stick with his own concepts despite adverse criticism or other people's opinions.

There followed a difficult four years in London, constantly moving from one lot of unpleasant digs to the next, being at one time housed by an artists' cooperative in near-derelict conditions. He found London, he says, grey and oppressive and this mood is reflected in his work of the time.

Jerry works on large canvases, on the whole, and with juxtapositions of sombre and bright colours and tones. His work has a distinctly medieval quality about it and, although he admits to many influences from Matisse to Munch, his main reference points are early illustrated manuscripts and Giotto. As was the case with Giotto, Jerry's work is 'humancentric,' because as he says, it is people and our relationships with them that is the basis of all our lives. One's initial response to his paintings may well be a good belly laugh but then as one looks harder, strange and difficult emotions begin to emerge.

These are not easy paintings, but they are powerful and arresting. There. is a silent tension about them and a feeling of painful anxiety; a distillation of the complexities of human relationships. Jerry is more inclined to be interested in 'mood' than realistic draughtsmanship but this only adds to their essential, dreamlike quality.

The paintings have a fairly rigid geometric structure because he feels that it is only within rigidity that he can explore his ideas and feelings. Some people have described his work as 'surreal' and there are certainly reoccurring symbols such as we have in our dreams. Open windows, falling objects, devilish animals, Turkish coffee pots and many more images appear time and again.

He will juggle with space and scale for psychological impact rather than mere representation. Jerry. works lots of paintings at once, going back over them, rediscovering and learning all the time, so that each block has an homogeneity about it. All of them have an intense stillness. Like flies caught in amber, we find his subjects caught and voyeuristically look in on their private worlds.

Jerry also works in collage. but at the moment he sees these as a related side-line and, through lack of time, the exhibition will be almost all oils on canvas.

He is indebted to Wolf at the Door for the encouragement that has made this exhibition possible. However, I have a feeling that this will be the first of many more to come: His work is not only powerful and individual but also very saleable, with a definite contemporary feel to it. He is certainly a painter to watch out for in the future and his exhibition is worth taking a look at.

Tarter

Robin Williamson

Martin Val Baker (November 1987).

Robin Williamson—old incredible, multi-instrumentalist, master storyteller, prolific songwriter, singer of songs, writer of TV scores, poet and non-driver arrived in Penzance in October as part of his British tour. Just before he went on stage, I talked to him about life on the road twenty years on.

MVB: *You are still not driving? (A trick question—Poets don't drive.)*
RW: No, there ought to be a law against me doing it—though I do have a learner's licence in my bag. (Still a Poet!).

Have words become more important than music for you?
I've been trying to make a mixture of the two, as others have done, Bob and Clive, for instance [Devereux and Palmer] I like the interplay between words and music.

Are you still sticking to harp, pipes and guitar?
I've been doing a lot of other stuff, scores, bits and pieces in the studio with synthesizers.

Isn't that cheating—using machines?
It's an awful handy short cut. A lot of these new synthesizers sound very much like the instruments when they go through small speakers but the actual live effect of a real instrument in a real room is quite a different thing. You are actually moving air around and there are people there ... it's a magical thing you don't get with a machine.

Real instruments for live performances—machines for recording?
You can't pretend that the machines aren't there, they have a function, they're marvellous and useful for certain things.

Are you still doing the storytelling?
Yes, I've done 25 of the stories on cassette and there is a book of them coming out soon; there is also a record for children called *Songs for Children of all ages.*

And 'Winter's Turning' I was very impressed by that.
That's a mixture of synthesizer and live instrumentalists.

Is it possible to take a group like that on the road anymore?
It's pretty hard in Britain. I'm trying to do it in Europe next summer, the musicians from *Winter's Turning* are in America so I'll probably put a band together here as I'm now based in Cardiff.

So you will go to the States to tour rather than vice versa?
I go to America this winter and in the early summer, other than that I'll be here.

Do you go to any exotic places—Australia, Japan?
I've been to Bermuda, Australia, Europe. Spain, Italy, Germany ... I recently did a piece of music for one of the top classical koto players in Japan—she recorded it in Bath earlier this year.

Do you mind the 'ex-Incredible String Band' label being used by promoters?
Not really, though it's been so long since the end of the ISB. It's not the way I would describe myself now; provided people like the label, it doesn't offend me. In fact we did 18 albums with the ISB and I've done more than 40 major things since then.

Can you see yourself playing on the same stage as Mike Heron again one day?
It's unlikely; when Mike plays, which is seldom, he mainly plays a much more Rock 'n Roll sound.

It's the style of music that's different?
It's an electric sound while I play a very acoustic and Celtic sound, I don't think we'd be frightfully compatible. I see him every so often, we get along fine, but musically we're as different as chalk and cheese.

But might it not be interesting—in the same way that three painters from the same art school might put on an exhibition after 20 years—to see what the three of you are doing musically, even though the styles maybe totally different?
I wouldn't object to that idea if there was the right place to do it.

Will there be more TV and film work?
Possibly; I'll be doing some work on the new George Lucas film next year, also I'm doing the new Mabignon in Cardiff with a cast of 90 and a three week run in a 2,000 seater hall next August.

Are there any new LPs in the pipeline?
I've just finished an album of my new songs, it's due out in the spring, no title as yet, with three Welsh musicians and a Welsh singer—Elaine Moore.

Can you actually do anything besides play music and tell stories?
To be quite honest I'm pretty poor at most other things; I tried working in a shop once and wasn't very good at that! I'm still able to work all over Britain and America ... as long as there are places to play ...

How long can you go on touring—will you still be doing it in another twenty years?
If nothing else changes and I still have my health and strength—yes I hope to be.

Where do you see yourself as a pensioner—where will you end up ... America, Wales, Scotland?
God alone knows! We were only talking about that today; occasionally I think about going back to Edinburgh, I quite like Cardiff, it definitely won't be America ... though having said that, you never know!

Travelling around all the time must be very difficult, you must become attached to some people, some places—and you know that you may never see them again.
That's the reason I like travelling.

So you have no commitments—no roots?
The planet. It's a bigger root than most peoples.

So you still find the business stimulating—you don't get bored yet?
No, I'm not bored! I'm definitely not bored—although we spent nine hours on the road yesterday, we usually find things to do, things to see ...

And you hope to come back to Cornwall again?
I'd love to, I really would!

For the latest news on books, albums and tapes available by Robin write to: Robin Williamson Productions, BCM 4797 London WC1N 3XX.

Kif Wood

Ashley Peters (October 1988)

"'I am essentially a lazy engineer,' to quote O'Donahue's fifth corollary of Murphy's Law, which says that if you've got a really difficult job to do, give it to a lazy man and he will find an easier way of doing it. This is the basis of how I design my guitars." Kif Wood.

Kif was born in Sussex in 1946. He went to Worthing Art College for four years, studying industrial design with engineering. He finished with an SIAD qualification in 1969. He became self-employed as an industrial design consultant. In designing, Kif has always been interested in understanding how a thing worked from start to finish, not just the outside package of things.

However, he was soon disillusioned with the design world and became a mechanic. Around this time, Kif wanted to make music and by chance in London met Dan Armstrong a well-known innovator in the field of making guitars and in amplification. He worked with him as an unpaid engineer. Together they came up with the then revolutionary sliding pick-up concept, sliding any-where under the strings between the neck and the bridge. Kif found he had a natural ability to understand musical instruments and the vibrating string. He didn't stay long in London and in 1971 came to Cornwall for a holiday, loved it and has stayed ever since.

He moved to Pendeen and started designing instruments, although self-taught. He took his engineering training and set himself a design brief to design a guitar from first principles. A period of designing and experimentation took place in the '70s, while he grew to understand the conversion of string energy into sound waves through the pump principle (the guitar is a pump).

He came up with some new concepts which have been incorporated into his guitars. He used to build his guitars as quickly as possible to see if his ideas worked, completely ignoring traditional techniques. This meant designing materials with which he could work, such as laminates and plywood's.

Although experiencing financial and other hardships during the '70s and early '80s, the more Kif got into this work the more he realised he wanted to make music and musical instruments. It became his vocation.

He persisted to make his instruments better and better and in 1985 at the Barbican, London, he had a first showing of his work with British and continental European guitar makers. It caused an amazing stir, because his guitars bore no resemblance to anything that anybody else was making. Everyone said that they couldn't work and what funny shapes they were, but when they played them, they came back very impressed and not only by the sound. They are well balanced, fit the body comfortably and the controls are easy to get at.

He specialises now in acoustic and electric basses and 12 strings. His acoustic basses are reputed to be the best available (to quote Simon Edwards from Fairground Attraction). Among his other customers are Marco Peroni (Adam and the Ants), Dave Pegg (Fairport Convention), Bill Nelson (Bebop Deluxe), Martin Kemp (Spandau Ballet) and the Dubrova Brothers, a Russian folk band.

Living now overlooking Perranuthnoe beach, Kif is making his latest six-string guitar in panels of bloodwood and solid ebony. The ebony is 265 years old—the piece sank off Cape Normandy, but it is not cracked and is an incredible piece of timber. It has taken Kif years to evolve these distinct guitar shapes. They are beautiful as whole forms. Acoustic shapes, in particular, are very adventurous. He evolved the shapes essentially from the lute soundboard—a rounded, elongated triangle—then found a way of holding them, hence the hooked cutaways to go over the knee.

The very large bass guitars are designed to produce a very low natural resonance; the small-bodied guitars have a bright rich sound with a long sustain. The unique construction of his designs allows him to use enormous variations of exotic timber and laminate colours that face the guitar at no extra expense. There is a great deal of matching and blending of the different coloured woods, which come from all over the world.

Kit designs and makes his own plywood for the backs and sides as a base and this economy is important to him, what with the destruction of the rain forests. In this way, he uses only a fraction of the quantity of exotic, decorative timber. A laminated timber/plywood is a dirty word in the music business, but it is incredibly stable, not subject to temperature and humidity as solid woods are.

He uses a lot of hard rosewoods and maple for the fretboarding, neck laminates and beadings. The soundboards on all the acoustics are white quarter-sawn sycamore. The decorative veneers he carefully selects from a timber merchant up the line, like the Japanese rippled ash he is putting on another new guitar, and ziricote on another. Ziricote is a Belizean hardwood which possesses an unbelievably beautiful pattern, from light yellow through to brown and black. When that guitar is finished, it will be stunning.

The range of colours of these timbers in his workshop vary from bright lemon yellow to purple to green to scarlet and maroon. He will put dyes on some woods only if it enhances the guitar. Some banded sycamore, when polished, looks like a metal finish

He is now putting custom-made pick-ups in all his acoustic guitars as standard, with contact mikes if people want them. This also fits in as part of the design and he is the first person to do it. The guitars are finished in cellulose, highly polished, satin or french polished or oiled. All the guitars he makes (apart from one or two of the solid guitars) have a revolutionary new bridging system. The advantage of this is that they are adjustable for height and intonation. You can adjust the tuning of the guitar exactly according to different weights, strings and so on.

Kif has been more adventurous than most with musical instruments. All credit to him. These new guitars will be on show in London at the Guitar Weekend '88 at the Polytechnic of Central London, the world's premier guitar show, on 8th and 9th October. In the near future he is taking his guitars to sell in Los Angeles, and taking a trip to Central and South America to look at timbers to purchase. If you're a serious music maker, then try one out for yourself.

Brenda Wootton

Martin Val Baker (February 1986)

Brenda Wootton, for many years known as 'Cornwall's first lady of song' has been forging a successful new career as an entertainer in the concert halls of France. Following her emergence from the folk club boom of the 'sixties, Brenda toured extensively throughout the British Isles and then, as the recession began to bite turned to Europe for bookings. During the Christmas break I found her working hard on a new project with the Cornish writer Richard Gendell, which is due for production later this year.

Surprisingly, Brenda was born in Wembley, *"much to my disgust"*, though she soon moved back to Cornwall with her family, living first at Ludgvan and later at Newlyn. Both her father (Penzance and church) and mother (Newlyn and chapel) were from well-established local families and thus she was surrounded by a legion of cousins from an early age—her grandfather 'Leather Ass' Ellery had been head groom at the Queen's Hotel in the days before the motorcar.

Brenda's first experiences as a performer were with a chapel choir in Newlyn where a tough choir master instilled in her the importance of thorough rehearsal before any public performance. Another influence at that time was the powerful oratory of the local ministers *"as dramatic as any Shakespearean ham"* who, as well as enlightenment, provided real entertainment for the children of Newlyn. Soon Brenda became involved with the local theatre groups performing regularly around Penwith, and from them learnt the basic rules of stagecraft. Often she worked a seven night week, acting, rehearsing, performing skits with a four-piece group called The Choughs or giving talks on acting around West Cornwall.-

In 1965, at the suggestion of her young daughter, Brenda and her husband John went to the Count House. folk club at Botallack which had recently been opened by Ian Todd. Brenda was amazed to hear "all those songs I didn't know" sung and played by the resident performers, *"those early Count House days were magic, it was that cold out there—and so innocent too. Cocoa cola and crisps, and everyone singing like mad—all-night sessions, sometimes till five in the morning."* Brenda and her family became regular visitors to the club and soon she was asked up on stage, *"though I didn't know any folk songs."* However, she had previously researched the verses of a song whilst performing with Madron Players and it was with this that she made her debut at the Count House—the song was 'Lamorna'.

Now a folk music addict. (and with the help of singer John the Fish), Brenda discovered more and more material by taping guest artists and listening to the fast proliferating output of folk revival records. With a lively, entertaining repertoire and Fish as her accompanist, Brenda began to get bookings further afield including a week in Norfolk arranged by Alex Atterson.

Around this time Brenda took over the organisation of the Count House, and over the next twelve years, as the club moved to St. Buryan (where it was renamed Pipers Folk) and Penzance, she built a national reputation for it through her shrewd booking policy. The club often ran for seven nights a week in the early 'seventies and Brenda also promoted concerts at St. John's Hall featuring Ralph McTell, Steeleye Span, Magna Carta *et al* whilst the club guests included the cream of the British folk scene.

In 1971, Brenda was invited to sing at the first Lorient Celtic Festival in Brittany and this led to a series of bookings at other Celtic Festivals. The Cornish Language Board decided to send her as their representative to the prestigious Killarney Festival in Ireland, but as there were no suitable songs in Cornish she had to take an English song and get it translated. This lead to a long and productive association with the Cornish scholar Richard Gendell, who over the years has produced more than 400 songs in Cornish for Brenda. At these very lively gatherings, Brenda finds a tremendous Celtic spirit abounds, much removed from the rather serious academic approach back in her own country where a rather precious attitude to the language prevails.

After 20 years in the music business, Brenda is now able to take things a little easier; there is no more sleeping on floors, or 500 mile drives on her frequent visits to France. Her very astute agent in Paris arranges flights, and she is met at the airport by a roadie who will drive her to the concert hall and later back to her hotel. Brenda performs only at concerts or for TV and Radio these days and although her nationality makes her a bit of an outsider, she has become a minor cult figure with a following ranging from teenagers to grandmothers. A handy spin-off from the French connection has been several tours of Canada (where her French TV shows are seen) including an appearance at the Montreal Jazz Festival and a week's booking in Ottawa—there are also plans to release a compilation album from the 23 LPs and 6 she has recorded. In France, Brenda has noticed the amount of pride and money that the authorities (at all levels) are prepared to invest in Culture, Sports and the Arts—a town the size of Penzance would have a professionally-run concert Hall/Theatre (with lighting engineers) and benefit from proper maintenance!

Nowadays, Brenda's material covers a wide spectrum of music including blues and vaudeville, which she is particularly adept at—*"it's lovely to howl out the big notes."* She feels, however, that she should not specialise and do, for instance, an album of blues numbers; her LPs, like her performances, will contain a cross-section of styles from church and semi-opera to vaudeville and Celtic. With performance, Brenda finds the spoken introduction as important theatrically as the song that follows it; if, for instance, she was given three minutes on TV, Brenda would use half that time to set the mood. She denies that she is an ambassador for Cornwall or indeed a messenger for women, *"I'm an entertainer who has learnt to survive in an extremely hard business in which the greatest compliment is to be called a professional performer—and I feel that I am one, right through to the fingertips."*

Fred Yates

Ashley Peters (August 1988)

"Having been brought up to a Northern way of life, it's hardships, plus the simple happiness by which one manages to survive. I have worked away unaware of time, and often without ambition, using painting as a stepping-stone through life, a stepping stone which has carried me over many obstacles and has brought me many friends and much happiness." Fred Yates.

There is a bit of theatre about the situation I find myself in: sitting down in Fred Yates' front room, watching him put on thin pink kitchen gloves and gleefully squeezing dollops of paint out of tubes onto his palette board. His hands are sore from mixing cement for a couple of days—he's fixing his house up. He is sitting down, too, opposite a blank white board. He is keen to get on and paint again with 'no holds barred,' feeling that he has nothing to lose. We begin the interview with a coastal view appearing on his board.

Born in Manchester in 1922, be became an insurance clerk. He served in the Grenadier Guards during the Second World War. Post war took him to a teaching course at Bournemouth and onto being an art teacher for 18 years. He retired from teaching and came to Fowey, where a new life started. There were many reasons for coming, but one was that you could buy a house for £3,500 in the mid-'60s, and live on a fiver a week. He also used to push a lawn mower to keep himself. He painted, selling some canvasses to holiday-makers. It was pretty hard going: He always paints for himself.

The major change came when he moved to Cape Cornwall five years ago. From selling to tourists in Fowey, local galleries in St Ives and Penzance were now taking his work and selling it for him and the financial pressures eased somewhat.

He marries painting up with living: He doesn't put painting before anything else, it falls into place. As he says, "My painting has to fit like a shell on a snail as part of my life."

If a house has to be done up, he does it up. He does not believe in making a god of anything.

Little ragbag figures are now appearing in the beach part of the picture. Quite a lot of white is being squeezed and mixed into the other colours. They are not unlike the exaggerated, expressionistic fairground colours which he loves, in particular the reds and blues. He takes care over the tonal values. He remembers Manchester as dull: He would colour his life by visiting fairgrounds, Punch and Judy shows and pantomimes, falling in love with the magical backcloths and the mechanics of it all.

He is considered in some quarters as being a little old-fashioned and nostalgic. Many of his paintings are a strange marriage between the 1930s and the up-to-date 1980s. Some of them have a French feel about them, in that their colours are clean, brilliant and exciting. He also has a great love of pattern. Sometimes in the streets when he's painting, on-lookers often say, "I don't understand the painting but, oh, what happy colours, Mr Yates."

He doesn't paint according to the books on colour theories. He admires other people's theories, but for him it takes all sorts to make a world.

He used to teach Women's Institute ladies near Polperro. When he first met them, they felt they would like to go to his painting classes, but they couldn't draw and that put them off. Well, he told them, he was the man to help them, because he painted without drawing. They did wonderfully well, he says.

He is still very disciplined and direct. These things, reminders of his days in the Guards, have never left him, but he is very gentlemanly and unassuming, if still terrified of authority.

A couple of ladies have now appeared in the painting, standing beside the seashore. They appear to be bare or pink-swimsuited, looking out toward the fishing boats.

His painting has really loosened up since he arrived in West Cornwall. He is less inhibited and more expansive showing more bravado. This freedom talks in his paintings.

Yates: "I don't always regard a painting, as just something that you hang upon a wall in the best parlour room. Someone said to me one day 'We put your painting up in the kitchen so we could look at it while we were doing the washing up.' That's nice."

For him, paintings shouldn't be too precious. "Some people say that they look at my painting everyday and laugh every time they see it. Or it calms them down. The nice thing is, you don't do it consciously with that in mind. It just happens that my paintings have these effects on some people.".

He thinks every artist's work is acceptable and has grown to like everything from very abstract to landscape and figurative. He likes to ring the changes, otherwise he gets bored. Being alert and explorative he is therefore, always off to somewhere to paint.

He is an outdoor painter, given the chance, but is equally at home indoors painting his imagined world. The only real grindstone is that he hasn't got a car. It takes him a lot of time to get to a place where he wants to paint. He has to walk or catch a bus and often spends five hours travelling to do two hours of painting.

Commissions for his paintings are more frequent now, one being for Esther Rantzen. It happens to be a portrait of her house and he has absolute freedom to be Fred Yates, to be tongue-in-cheek. He's handled this type of commission before, painting the people of Hampstead walking past a house, a shop or an office, some of them pushing prams. Basically, he feels they want a little record of their homes before they move on and to show their children.

Another ragbag figure has just come into this coastal picture, pushing a pram on the beach.

Yates: "I suppose what I paint is Manchester people on holiday, I take them with me."

Frustrated by the gloves, he's taken them off to put in finer details by brush and smudges by finger. Some foliage is going in at the bottom and near the corners.

That's almost it. The frame goes around the painting, he stands back for the first time and gets a surprise, a buzz.

His paintings can be seen around many local galleries. Some are in Newlyn Orion, New Craftsman and Wills Lane Gallery, St Ives.